Pı

INTO THE BLUE

"*Into the Blue* provides an exceptional guide to driving fulfillment, passion, and productivity in the workplace. Sri Chellappa does a masterful job of applying the ancient Japanese concept of ikigai to develop a framework for matching the person to the job and the job to the company. The book is filled with engaging stories from Chellappa's extraordinary personal business journey, supported by well-researched studies and renowned experts. This book provides tangible strategies and practices that can be immediately implemented to foster a work environment where passion, purpose, and performance converge, and employees thrive. If you are seeking a practical guide that transcends theory and delivers real results, *Into the Blue* is a must-read."

—Gordon Rapkin, 5X CEO

"In *Into the Blue*, Sri Chellappa masterfully navigates the intersection of ancient philosophy and modern workplace dynamics. Through captivating storytelling, real-life anecdotes, and actionable strategies, this book reveals how embracing the principles of ikigai can revolutionize every employee's productivity and their job fulfilment. A must-read for anyone committed to fostering a work environment where passion, purpose, and performance converge."

—Melissa Widner, CEO, Lighter Capital

"*Into the Blue* reconciles two seemingly contradictory concepts—ancient wisdom and the modern workplace. It is packed with practical examples, real-world insights, common sense perspectives, and creative ways of rethinking the way people live and work. This book is essential reading for any leader who wants to drive top organizational performance and maximize individual fulfillment at the same time."

—Ian Ziskin, president, EXec EXcel Group; former CHRO, Northrup Grumman

"*Into the Blue* introduces us to the principles of ikigai, where author Sri Chellappa masterfully fuses ancient wisdom with modern workplace dynamics. With practical insights and real-world examples, the author illuminates how aligning individual passions and strengths with organizational goals can elevate teams to peak performance and individual fulfillment at work. This book is essential reading for leaders and team members seeking to create purpose-driven workplaces where employees can thrive."

—Edie Goldberg, PhD, founder and president, E. L. Goldberg & Associates; board chair, SHRM Foundation

"As modern workers find themselves grappling with an unprecedented existential challenge, Sri Chellappa offers a timely and practical blueprint for finding purpose in one's professional life. *Into the Blue* is a primer on how to intentionally construct people practices that help workers discover and align with their most integral selves. In doing so, Chellappa has struck the balance between economics and ethos that has become requisite in our new world of work."

—Matt Poepsel, PhD, VP and the Godfather of Talent Optimization, The Predictive Index

"In *Into the Blue*, Srikant Chellappa offers a powerful road map for transforming the workplace by aligning individual passions and organizational goals. Through practical insights and real-world examples, this book empowers leaders and team members to create purpose-driven environments where everyone thrives—with the timeless wisdom of ikigai. If you're committed to fostering growth and success within your organization, this essential read provides actionable strategies to revolutionize productivity and job satisfaction."

—Drew Fortin, CEO, Lever Talent

INTO

THE

BLUE

IMPLEMENTING **IKIGAI PHILOSOPHY**
TO CREATE A MEANINGFUL WORKPLACE

SRI CHELLAPPA

AN INC.
ORIGINAL

An Inc. Original
New York, New York
www.anincoriginal.com

This work is being published under the An Inc. Original imprint by an exclusive arrangement with *Inc. Magazine*. *Inc. Magazine* and the Inc. logo are registered trademarks of Mansueto Ventures, LLC. The An Inc. Original logo is a wholly owned trademark of Mansueto Ventures, LLC.

Distributed by River Grove Books

Design and composition by Greenleaf Book Group
Cover design by Greenleaf Book Group

Publisher's Cataloging-in-Publication data is available.

Print ISBN: 978-1-63909-044-0

eBook ISBN: 978-1-63909-045-7

First Edition

Dedicated to my daughter, Saachi
(a.k.a. Saachiko) "The blessed one."

CONTENTS

INTRODUCTION

I n the fast paced modern world, we often find ourselves on a relent-
less pursuit of success in our work and life, navigating through the
complexities of life with a fervent determination to achieve our goals.
A significant portion of our journey is dedicated to our work—more
than 90,000 hours, to be precise. These hours are the precious time upon
which we build our careers, aspirations, and dreams. They encompass
our most energetic, productive, and youthful years until we transition
into retirement or cease working for various reasons. When we realize
that these waking hours, spent at work, are among our most precious,
it therefore becomes essential to explore whether we are living our best
work life in those invaluable hours we commit to it.

I was inspired by the Okinawan people of Japan, who are famed for
their longevity but also their overall purpose-driven approach to their
lives. They live exceptionally long and meaningful lives, and a substantial
part of this longevity can be attributed to their unique approach to life,
work, and relationships—an approach they call *ikigai*. Ikigai encapsu-
lates the essence of finding true purpose and fulfillment in life.

In its simplest form, ikigai is the convergence of four critical elements: passion, skill, mission, and vocation. *Passion* is the inner fire
that stirs your soul, fills your heart with joy, and makes each day a
meaningful journey. It's what you love, what you're enthusiastic about,

and what gets you out of bed in the morning. *Skill* represents the expertise you possess or continue to cultivate and refine over time. It is the foundation of your competence, enabling you to excel in your chosen pursuits. *Mission* guides you toward contributing to the world in a meaningful way. It's about addressing real-world problems and needs, making a positive impact, and leaving a lasting legacy. *Vocation* bridges the gap between your passion, skill, and mission by allowing you to earn a livelihood from your chosen endeavors. It's the practical aspect that sustains you financially while you pursue your purpose.

The Okinawan approach to ikigai presents an opportunity for us to rethink the way we perceive our work. It offers a blueprint for infusing our professional lives with purpose and fulfillment, aligning our daily efforts with something greater than ourselves. My personal journey in search of purpose in my work has profoundly shaped the contents of this book. I firmly believe that it is not only possible but essential for each and every one of us to discover our ikigai in the realm of our careers.

Whether you find yourself in a seemingly mundane role, such as a parking lot attendant, or at the helm of an organization as a CEO, the desire to find purpose and meaning in our work is universal. As a follower of Viktor Frankl's philosophy of purpose-driven life rather than the pursuit of happiness, I have come to understand that our inherent human nature craves purpose and growth. It's not merely the pursuit of comfort or perpetual happiness; it's about having a profound purpose that fuels personal development and nurtures our passions. This is what gets us through challenging times and fuels our inner self to push through adversity.

Leaders and organizations hold a unique responsibility in this journey. It is not only an ethical but also a fiduciary responsibility for them to cultivate cultures that empower individuals to find purpose at work. When leaders create environments where people can align their passions, develop their skills, contribute to a mission, and sustain themselves through their vocations, everyone benefits. It is a win-win scenario, where individuals bring their best selves to work, and organizations thrive as a result.

This book is a culmination of almost three decades of my personal journey through various organizations, including over eight years at the helm of Engagedly. Along the way, I have developed a profound appreciation for the many organizational leaders who have influenced my path—those I have worked for, worked with, or sought guidance from. My exploration of the principles of ikigai led me to a deep appreciation of how these principles align with the practices of many organizational leaders and employees who have managed to lead purposeful work lives.

My primary goal in writing this book is to provide a framework based on my interpretation of ikigai. I aim to demonstrate how these principles can be applied to the workplace, creating thriving environments where individuals find purpose and organizations flourish. It's a road map for both personal and professional fulfillment, a guide to discovering the sweet spot where passion, skill, mission, and vocation converge.

In this book, we will delve deep into the profound wisdom of ikigai. We will explore how it can reshape not only our careers but our lives as well. It is my hope that this exploration will inspire you and the people you lead to seek your and their ikigai, both within and outside the confines of work, and in doing so, unlock the true potential of a life filled with meaning and purpose.

1

THE IKIGAI BLUE ZONE
AND WORKPLACE

Just possibly, ikigai makes a Peter Pan of all of us. And that is not necessarily a bad thing. Let us all be twelve years old! Youthfulness of mind is important in ikigai, but so [are] commitment and passion, however seemingly insignificant your goal.

—Ken Mogi

In this chapter, we will explore concepts from the ikigai blue zones and how they can be applied to the workplace, where there are different stakeholders, including the organization, managers, and employees.

There are three major concepts of the ikigai blue zone that can lead to a more fulfilling life. Spoiler alert—it is not seeking happiness! Happiness is a fleeting concept that can come and go depending on the day and the work you are doing. Fulfillment at work is the true feeling one should be striving for. When an organization and its management across all levels successfully align their work culture, process, and people with providing more fulfilling roles for those people, then there is alignment between the organization and its people. The idea behind providing an ikigai workplace is to help you be more effective and productive. The concepts of ikigai at work are:

- Finding a sense of purpose
- Finding the right balance between passion, fun, and growth
- Feeling respected and appreciated by those around you

The workplace ikigai zones are illustrated in Figure 1.1, which explains this in more detail.

The outer circle defines the organizational culture, which is primarily driven by its leadership and management. Without a culture that supports its managers to be flexible with their people—giving their people voice and agency in their careers and a focus on not only career but also personal growth—managers will fail to build an ikigai workplace in

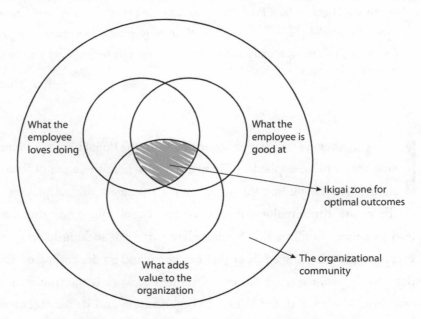

Figure 1.1. The workplace ikigai zones. The area where the three circles intersect at the center is the ikigai blue zone for optimal outcomes.

their teams. This work environment actually has a much greater impact on the overall fulfillment and sense of purpose of the individual than we might expect. This outer circle overrules the impact of the individual circles of work activities. Organizations need to pay special attention to building a strong and satisfying work culture to succeed in the long run.

The three smaller circles that form the core of the ikigai workplace framework are where managers can work with their people to find the alignment that leads to the most fulfilling and productive work. Speaking in broad terms, and seeing it from an employee's perspective, their work can be categorized in these three areas:

- SKILL: Work that they are exceptionally good at
- DESIRE: Work that they are interested in doing
- NEED: Work that is valuable to the organization

We will call this the SDN, and these areas represent the framework of the ikigai approach for the development of a fulfilling workplace design.

In terms of *skill*, most people can become extremely proficient and excel at a task as a result of doing it for a very long time, or because they have a natural or innate ability to do that task well. Skill development is a priority for a lot of organizations as our workplaces continue to evolve. It is quite possible to develop a skill in an area one is working in by learning from different sources and getting mentors or coaches. But even so, that does not imply that they want to continue doing that work. There are a lot of reasons for this. Maybe they get bored, or they don't find it challenging anymore. Even people who have what many consider dream jobs, such as celebrities or sports figures, have felt this way about their careers. While having a skill certainly makes one's work less onerous, it cannot by itself be fulfilling to an employee if there are other elements missing in the ikigai framework.

When it comes to *desire*, people are generally interested and motivated in doing work that gives them energy; this work is something they can push themselves to do even when they are exhausted, or not in the best state mentally. This is the type of work or activity that is often described as being "in the zone." The experience of being in the zone tends to give you a sense of ecstasy and total concentration, and often makes the activity seem effortless. Psychologist Mihaly Csikszentmihalyi, a former researcher and professor at Claremont Graduate University in California, famously coined the term *flow*, which he describes as the immersive moment when a person is completely involved in an activity for its own sake. Mihaly Csikszentmihalyi asks, "What makes a life worth living?" He notes that money cannot make us happy, nor can power. He goes on to say people who learn to control inner experience will be able to determine the quality of their lives, which is as close as any of us can come to being happy. He looks to those who find pleasure and lasting satisfaction in activities that bring about a state of "flow."

It is hard to pinpoint what can create desire, since one's desire for a certain type of work can be a chore to another. And sometimes, a chore can become a desire as one sees success in their work, as they get more skilled, or get appreciated for that work. Sometimes it's a mindset shift, where you can start looking at this work that is hard and not desirable as a challenge you need to overcome.

Need is the third and last part of SDN, and in terms of employment is the one that has the greatest value to an organization. It is also, generally speaking, the most important from an organization's point of view. This is basically where an organization has a need driven by their strategy and operations. Most organizations lean heavily on this circle without emphasis on the other circles since this is the priority driven by the leadership, which percolates to different levels of management.

This creates a particularly challenging situation for an organization because setting an objective without getting its people aligned to that purpose does not lead to long-term success. The question they have to ask themselves is, *How can we get our people to experience a state of flow while at the same time fulfilling our organization's needs, which will add value to us and further our mission?*

The area where the three circles of the SDN intersect is the ikigai blue zone for optimal outcomes. This is where the work being done by the employee involves the skill of the employee and their desire in that work and where the organization has the need because that work is aligned to the organizational objectives. The goal of every manager and employee is to work together to find work alignment that falls in this intersection.

However, there are multiple zones of work an employee could be in. Broadly speaking, they are broken down into three zones: red, purple, and blue. And each of these zones is subdivided further. Both the red and purple each have three zones, and blue has one zone. For the purposes of this book, we are only considering the zones where at least one of the three areas—skill, desire, and need—exists in the role. The zone of work where none of the three elements exist is evidence of a broken organization and management. There are bigger problems that probably manifest in that work culture.

For clarity, the size of these zones is not representative of their overall value and is for illustration purposes only. For instance, the blue zone might actually comprise far more work items than all of the other zones combined, or one of the purple zones might have more work items than the others. Conceptually, they are zones of work that represent where an employee experiences a certain level of competency, interest, and value (or lack thereof).

Let's explore these zones in more detail.

RED ZONES

The red zones are the areas of work for an employee where only one of the three elements is true. The majority of their work is missing two out of three elements in their day-to-day work. We will explore each of these three red zones in more detail.

Red Zone 1

I have always loved building mathematical models. It probably comes from my love of probability and statistics. In one of my earlier jobs at a major company, I would build all these models to show different types of return on investments on internal R&D projects. My manager loved it, and we would go into management meetings to showcase these models to prove that the project we were working on was worth investing in.

There was a lot of optimism going into those meetings. However, it was evident after several such meetings that for most of the people in the room, their eyes glazed over when I would describe these models. While I loved building these models, it was clearly a counterproductive

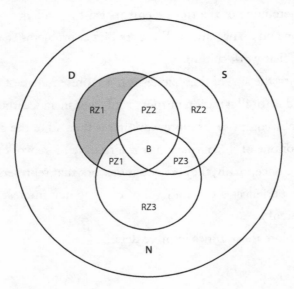

exercise because, more often than not, these models were wrong. They never took into account the human factor in using these devices or technology we wanted to build.

These models were neither skillful (primarily because they were incorrect) nor were they something my organization wanted to see. While I loved building these incorrect models, they were a big waste of time, money, and energy. I was working in red zone 1: desire alone.

Red zone 1 is where the employee absolutely loves what they are doing, which generally leads to more satisfaction, fulfillment, and a sense of accomplishment. Oftentimes, this doesn't even feel like work—it feels more like fun. But even though the employee is involved in activities that they love doing, they, unfortunately, may not be very skilled or talented in this particular area of work, and as a result their work adds little to no value to the organization. Wasting valuable employee time is one thing, but that is amplified if the work is creating errors that lead to loss of productivity and require additional hours to correct.

Red Zone 2

Red zone 2 is where the employee is working in the area they are good at but not necessarily interested in and not necessarily needed by the organization. The employee is not too keen on continuing to do the work, and the organization doesn't see much benefit to it either.

Red zone 2 is an area where one finds themselves if they have been working in a role or an activity for years but eventually lose interest in it and find themselves making a lot of mistakes. Many people get bored of doing the same job, as it offers no challenge or personal growth. Even if it were valuable work to the organization, if the employee is not engaged or interested, they might not be very productive, or maybe they'll be prone to errors.

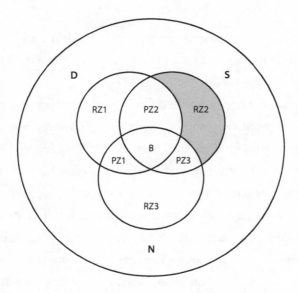

Much like the work in red zone 1, the organization may not see the point of the work, or the project may be missing key pieces that would make it useful. Or it may just be busy work, using the worker's skills for no discernible purpose.

Wendy Hamilton, CEO of TechSmith, a leading software developer of tools such as Camtasia and Snagit, says, "When the only utility of a job is a paycheck, it's an obligation not an opportunity. The biggest driver of employee disengagement is the lack of a purpose other than a paycheck."[1]

At this point, no one is winning: The employee is not getting any satisfaction from their role, and the organization is getting nothing useful to move their objective forward.

You'll note that these are the same problems encountered in red zone 1, but they have a different cause. However, it has the same result in that the work ultimately ends up being of no value for the organization. And sometimes, this red zone 2 in many ways is worse than red zone 1 since neither the organization nor the employee derives any pleasure or productive outcomes from this work.

Red Zone 3

Red zone 3 is where the organization benefits from the work product, but the employee neither enjoys nor is particularly interested in the work. Although the project may be of great value for the organization, the employees working within this zone tend to show little interest, and they lack the required skill to adequately do the job.

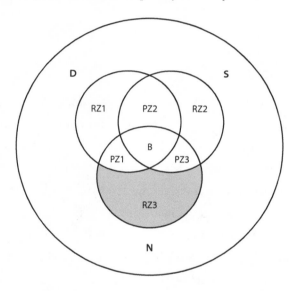

In my two decades of managing people and working with different teams, I have come across teams where red zone 3 is flashing brighter than the Las Vegas Strip, especially as the organizations get bigger and more people than necessary have been added to teams due to management vanity. I would see people doing subpar work in their role. For example, the design work might be completely uninspiring, or the Excel model they built is full of errors. To cap it off, they are completely uninterested in getting better or learning that skill because this work is not something that excites them. In many such instances, it is inertia that keeps them in their role and management that is not paying attention to building a high-performing team.

However, as is the case with many organizations, this eventually resolves itself in a way where there is little value creation for the organization or the employees' lives. This zone creates the perfect environment for rapid employee turnover, either by choice or by the organization. This type of work environment is also a breeding ground for bad managers, who find it easy to stay and scapegoat department problems on the employees.

PURPLE ZONES

In visiting different cities and parking in different parking lots, I would often make an observation about the job of a parking lot attendant or the person sitting inside a box at the toll booth. I would try to put myself in their position and visualize how I would feel if I was doing that eight to ten hours a day, day in and day out. It would not be a stretch to say that I would probably end up institutionalized. And yet, we see these humans on a daily basis. They are often good at their job, considering it is not a particularly high-skill role, and there are enough systems in place to help them do their work effectively. It is also of value to the business, as without these roles or high levels of automation, they would not be profitable. I doubt anyone thinks of the role of parking lot attendant as a desirable job, or one that they would enjoy. And the data show that only about 4 percent of the people in these roles find any meaning in their job.[2] Effectively, 96 percent of these people are working the majority of the time in a purple zone.

The purple zone is where we, as humans, must perform an activity that is necessary for us to make everything else work right. On an individual level, this entails activities such as brushing our teeth, going to the gym, and eating right. In a work environment, this can translate to keeping your workspace maintained, organized, and clean. Some employees really enjoy these activities; however, these tasks can become a demotivator for the employee or a detriment to the organization when a large majority of activities are in the purple zone.

As is the case with red zones, there are three purple zones. It is also where two work zones overlap. Fortunately, or unfortunately, most people end up working in purple zones much of the time. It is not necessarily the worst place for an employee to be, but these activities need to be balanced with work in the blue zones to be more fulfilling.

Purple Zone 1

This is the zone where an employee's activities are characterized by things the employee loves doing—things that the organization values—but is not particularly good at. On the surface, this zone appears to be a benign place for the employee to be. However, the organization might have a completely different perspective on this. While the individual is certainly working on something that is of value to the organization,

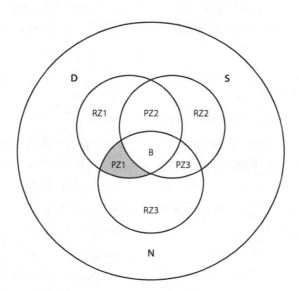

and this activity is something that the management clearly needs, it is unfortunately not something that the employee is good at.

To give you an example, let's say an organization has a clear need for marketing and branding, and one of their employees has an interest and enthusiastically wants to do this for the organization; it certainly appears on the surface to be a good fit of desire and need. But if the individual is not skilled in that area, the organization risks the messaging and branding falling flat, in the best-case scenario, and confusing the buyer, in the worst-case scenario.

Either scenario is bad, but the second one could potentially affect the organization's growth. This invariably will lead to one of two things happening: Either the individual will have to learn the necessary marketing and branding skills so as to add value to the work (which will take time), or the organization will need to replace the individual with someone who already has the necessary skills.

Depending on the path the organization takes, a purple zone could lead to a dead end for the individual's career, or they could move into the blue zone by gaining the required skills for the task. We will address movement to the blue zones from purple zones in a later chapter.

Purple Zone 2

This is a zone where the employee's activities are characterized by things the employee loves doing—things they are particularly good at but things that the organization does not value. From the organization's standpoint, this purple zone is arguably the worst of the three purple zones. The organization is paying for the individual to do this activity, but not realizing any value from the activities that exist in this zone. However, it's not all bad for the organization and, in fact, could be positive for them. As we previously discussed, it is not necessary for all activities to be in the

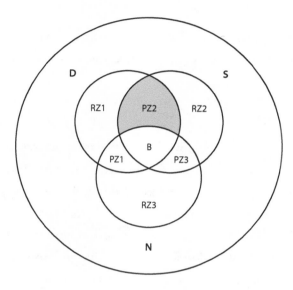

blue zone. If, from an organization's perspective, the majority of the work is in favorable zones for the organization, then allowing the individual to partake in some of the activities that may seem to add little value to the organization may be a great motivator for the individual to stay engaged and find some level of joy in their job. Having motivated employees alone adds value to both the employee and the organization. Allowing employees some time to pursue less productive activities will reduce stress and give them an opportunity to recharge. This can also be a way for organizations to reduce absenteeism due to burnout or illness.

Google and 3M famously give time off for personal projects that people want to pursue, which, on the surface, do not seem to provide any value for the companies, but several innovations have come from such endeavors. It would be foolish to think that innovations will always be the end result, but completely cutting off these nonproductive activities that exist in this zone can, in the long run, actually be detrimental to the broader success of the organization, resulting in demotivation of employees, burnout, and loss of productivity. Simply put, allowing employees to occasionally pursue nonproductive activities that they enjoy can lead to innovation that ultimately benefits the organization.

Purple Zone 3

This is a zone where the employee's activities are characterized by things they are particularly good at and things that the organization values, but things the employee does not find joy in doing. This zone is a recipe for high employee turnover if the individual finds that the majority of their work is in this area. This can greatly affect an employee's attitude toward their job and can lead to sloppy work, resulting in errors. This not only impacts the employee but the organization as well.

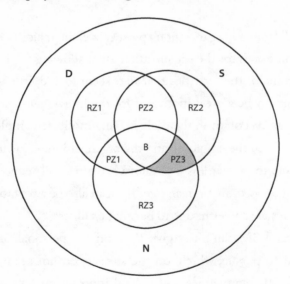

Fortunately, the work environment has evolved over the years. Many organizations have adopted an appreciation for focusing more on what the individual wants to work on. This, coupled with the fact that employees have much greater power in finding the job they want, has led to this zone losing its prevalence.

In a recent survey, only about 20 percent of employees said they are satisfied with their company as a place to work.[3] However, it is important to note that there are many activities that all organizations have that absolutely cannot be avoided. Some of these activities are like brushing your teeth, so yes, in many jobs you may not like filling in your timesheets (which requires no particular skill) or submitting your expense reports on time, but it is necessary to do those activities for any organization to properly function. This zone becomes more impactful to general demotivation and disengagement if the majority of the work is in the area the employee does not want to do, and they find themselves only doing it for a paycheck. Some jobs are inherently susceptible to this zone, like being a parking lot attendant, inventory clerk, or cashier.

We will discuss in future chapters what qualities in a job actually give joy and fulfillment to the individual. Most of us have a preconception of what these are, but you may be surprised that they are not as obvious as they may seem, and it is possible to find joy in work that may seem meaningless to many people. The answer to that lies in circle E, the work environment, which is a critical element in the overall success of an organization.

KEY TAKEAWAYS

- Fulfillment at work is more important than seeking happiness; it leads to a more sustainable sense of purpose.

- Three key concepts of ikigai at work are finding a sense of purpose by balancing passion for work, developing skill growth, and aligning with organizational strategic needs.

- The SDN framework represents the core of the ikigai approach for designing fulfilling workplaces. *Skill* refers to being proficient in a task, *desire* relates to being interested and motivated, and *need* is the work valuable to the organization.

- The outer circle signifies organizational culture, driven by leadership and management, which significantly impacts individual fulfillment.

- Red zones are areas where an employee's work lacks two or more of the key elements. Red zone 1 is when an employee loves their work but lacks skill and alignment to the organizational strategic needs, leading to potentially counterproductive outcomes. Red zone 2 occurs when an employee is skilled but uninterested in their work, which can result in boredom and mistakes, and is unaligned with the organizational needs. Red zone 3 involves work that benefits the organization but lacks interest and skill on the part of the employee, often leading to low value creation and high turnover.

- Purple zones are activities that are necessary but may not be particularly enjoyable or aligned with individual skills. Purple zone 1 involves doing work that an employee loves and is needed by the organization but lacks skill in, posing potential risks. Purple zone 2 entails work an employee loves and is skilled at but may not be highly valued by the organization. However, it can have motivational benefits. Purple zone 3 comprises work an employee is skilled at and is valued by the organization but doesn't bring joy, which can lead to demotivation and errors.

2

WHAT THE PERSON
IS GOOD AT

You must immerse yourself in your work. You have to fall in love with your work . . .
You must dedicate your life to mastering your skill. That's the secret of success.

—Chef Jiro

t the age of five, Giuliano Stroe set a Guinness World Record for the fastest ten-meter hand-walk with a weight ball between his legs. At the age of six, he broke the world record for the number of ninety-degree push-ups, an exercise that begins in a handstand position and then involves lowering one's body to a horizontal position without letting one's feet touch the ground, then returning to a handstand position. Between 1998 and 2005, Tiger Woods made the cut in 142 consecutive events to break the PGA TOUR record. In 1988, Steffi Graf became the first tennis player to achieve the Golden Slam by winning all four major singles titles and the Olympic gold medal in the same calendar year. Were these accomplishments all due to innate skill, or were they the right circumstances, where the individual's drive to excel was nourished?

Some people appear to simply be born with a great level of skill. However, for the rest of us mere mortals, we become proficient at something because we develop a passion and interest for it. Genetics and environmental factors can certainly play a part in making us more skilled at a task than the average individual, but generally it comes from drive, hard work, and repetition. Several studies have shown that most of us can get moderately successful if we focus on a specific area, either due to an encouraging environment in which a skill is reinforced (e.g., Asians with math or the Williams sisters with tennis), or because we develop a passion for that subject. At some point, after years of practice and time in a job, we tend to get good at that job.

It might be difficult if you are 5'6" to become a world-class basketball player (although Spud Webb did it!), but most people can get proficient at anything if they have the right environment and put enough time into it.

In his landmark book, *Developing Talent in Young People*, Benjamin Bloom, a professor of education at the University of Chicago, showed that most people who achieved world-class success did so because of the environment they were in—supportive parents, great coaches, and time dedicated to the activity.[1] In the research study "The Role of Deliberate Practice in the Acquisition of Expert Performance," published in 1993 in *Psychological Review*, the authors state,

> *The most cited condition concerns the subjects' motivation . . . to improve their performance . . . The subjects should receive immediate informative feedback and knowledge of results of their performance. The subjects should repeatedly perform the same or similar tasks.*

When these conditions are met, practice improves accuracy and speed of performance . . .[2]

And of course, there is the famous book *Outliers*, by Malcolm Gladwell, where he introduces the 10,000-hour rule, which states that it takes about that much time of intense practice to achieve a level of mastery in a particular activity.[3] However, other studies dispute this, saying the amount of hours Gladwell lists is completely arbitrary and that he dismisses other key ingredients, such as having a good teacher and the quality of the practice instead of the time spent practicing.

The point here is that most people with reasonable abilities can get good—and can get really good—at their job or a skill they want to acquire.

HOW BEING GOOD RELATES TO THE IKIGAI ZONES

We will refer back to this important aspect as we discuss the mechanics of the journey one takes from purple zone 1, where an employee has a strong desire to do a particular task that aligns with the organizational need, but the employee is weak on the necessary skill the task requires. It may be convenient, as a manager, to move that person to a different role or give them a different set of activities instead of actively investing in the employee's growth. However, it can become an exciting journey for the employee if they are provided the necessary resources, experience, or coaching to allow them to excel in those areas they enjoy that are also valuable to the organization. So, when there is an alignment of skill and desire, there is passion and better outcomes at work, which, in turn, leads to a high rating on the organizational need.

In purple zone 2, a person has the right skills and the desire to continue doing those activities that they have skills in. Finding a role that gives them both is a dream for many people. However, they may find themselves doing work in areas the organization finds little value in. In many cases, it may be the team they are part of. A conversation between the manager and the employee may lead to a role where they find themselves more aligned to the organization's needs and objectives.

Red zone 2 is where one is good at a certain skill but has no desire to continue to work in a role or activities related to the skill they have. And the organization doesn't have a need for that skill in furthering its organizational objectives; it will be evident that it is a skill that has little purpose for the individual or the organization. Fortunately, most employees will not find themselves in this zone in their roles at their organization. However, it is important to note that a person with a certain skill can often find an adjacent skill that might give them both marketability as well as desire to work on those roles.

When I was in tenth grade, personal computers were all the rage. Even though I did not possess one myself, I found myself learning how to program in Basic and Fortran, and I eventually became quite good at it. Fast forward to a few years later, and even though I had skills in these programming languages, I had no desire to continue to work in them, and most organizations did not need these specific skills in any case. However, I found myself really enjoying learning new programming languages, like Visual Basic and C/C++, which were more aligned with what organizations needed.

Ultimately, people become good at something because, at some point in their lives, they wanted to be good at these activities. However, realizing that one can move on to adjacent skills that can reignite passion and their marketability to organizations can lead people to work that is more fulfilling.

In both these cases, the manager plays an important role in understanding and actively collaborating with the employee to find the path that leads to a blue zone.

CONFIRMING SKILLS

But how does one know if they are good at their job, or even a particular skill? This is often a mystery and debated between the individual, their manager, and sometimes their peers. So, it is important to benchmark *good*, to some extent, from an objective standard, not a subjective one. Most people think they are better than they actually are at many tasks. For example, several studies have shown that more than 90 percent of US drivers consider themselves to be better than the median driver, which is mathematically impossible.[4] It would be interesting to find out who the other 10 percent humble humans are, but that's a subject for a different day.

Similar studies have been replicated multiple times across time and a variety of subjects with startling results that show a cognitive bias whereby people with less expertise, or experience, tend to overestimate their ability or knowledge. It is so consistent that there is a name for this: the Dunning–Kruger Effect. According to a research study published by the *Journal of Personality and Social Psychology*, Justin Kruger and David Dunning suggested that across many intellectual and social domains it is the poorest performers who hold the least accurate assessments of their skill and performances, grossly overestimating how well their performances stack up against those of their peers.[5] For example, students performing in the bottom 25 percent among their peers on tests of grammar, logical reasoning, and humor tended to think that they are performing above the sixtieth percentile. In fact, to carry it one step further, studies have gone on to show that the *less* competent one is, the *more* they overestimate their abilities. That means that sometimes when an employee thinks they are really good at something, they actually may not be. And the inverse can also be true; when a person says that they are not that good at a skill or competency, they may be underestimating themselves.

Assessing how "good" someone is at something can be difficult unless they are in an activity that maintains statistical comparisons—like many athletic professions—or has concrete results—like various jobs that would fall into blue-collar categories. However, there is no universally accepted objective measure in many organizational activities, which can make it troublesome in assessing how good someone is at a task. This is especially true in areas where the measurements are vague, say, for example, an understanding of science or leadership.

In an organization, therefore, it becomes important to define *good* with an objective measurement. This will vary from organization to organization, of course. For example, let's take the skill of design. Measuring what is *good* design for a magazine ad is different from *good* design for an online ad.

Knowing when someone is good at a task is a skill in and of itself and is a skill every manager and leader should aspire to get good at.

Gordon Rapkin, a five-time CEO, says, "You have to pay attention to the employee's body language and enthusiasm quotient. Sometimes you can spot what gets them going and focus on coaching them to pursue their passions."[6]

There are a few ways to tell when an employee is good at a job, the first being that they are typically sought after in the organization for their advice. This individual generally seeks active feedback on their performance from others. They consistently achieve or exceed their goals, and their broader work outcomes show consistent achievement. A manager's role then becomes to use and highlight these tools to define *good* not only for themselves and the organization, but also for the individual.

One way organizations can identify an individual's strengths is by conducting an effective 360-degree evaluation/feedback (also known as multi-rater feedback, multi-source feedback, or multi-source assessment), a process where feedback is gathered from an employee's subordinates, peers, colleagues, and supervisors, as well as a self-evaluation by the employee themselves. Such feedback can also include, when relevant, feedback from external sources who interact with the employee, such as customers and suppliers or other interested stakeholders. A well-developed 360-degree evaluation paired with a strengths-based assessment can be very powerful to help identify and focus on the strengths and skills of an employee.

One of the popular assessments is the CliftonStrengths assessment, by Gallup, which focuses on an individual's strengths as a foundation to build on. Paired with the 360-assessment, this enables the manager to have future-focused discussions on their employees' strengths to help build confidence and align their work to those strengths.

Signs of Proficiency

Once you've identified someone's "good" skills, you and your organization can then align them to roles that put those skills to better use. A person who is good at their job or the skill they are practicing will typically spend extra time putting forth the effort to master their skill even more. For example, top athletes or musicians don't sit around and wait for their next event; they are deliberately practicing between events to better hone the skills that got them to where they are to begin with. Michael Jackson—undeniably one of the greatest pop stars of our generation—continued to intentionally practice for many days before a show, as can be seen in the popular documentary *This Is It*.[7]

Matt Poepsel, a performance optimization expert with the organization Predictive Index, says this about identifying proficiency and potential in an individual:

When I'm evaluating an employee's capabilities, I look for their energy and results. The results are nonnegotiable, but if the employee is stretching or doesn't enjoy the effort it took to produce it, there's not a natural strength there. When the energy flows naturally and the individual is almost surprised that I'm surprised at how effortless they make it seem, that's a great sign.

I once managed a young woman who had a great eye for user experience with regard to various software interfaces. When I made an observation that she seemed to have a natural eye for work-flows, she responded, "Oh really? It just seems logical to me." Several months later, I transitioned her into a product management role where she excelled.[8]

Individuals who put forth this effort tend to get more feedback. This seems counterintuitive, but people who are good will get more feedback because others can see the potential of how much better that person can be. Getting more feedback (specifically, constructive feedback) means the person giving the feedback sees an individual's promise to be even better in that role or task.

Those who are good at their job typically will not go around gloating or boasting, because they don't have to; others will do this for them by directly telling them and everyone else at the organization how good they are. There is a popular saying that states, "People who are average tell others how good they are, whereas people who are great will have others say how good they are." People who are good will also not display the Dunning–Kruger Effect in that particular skill or area of expertise. So, listen for the whispers and feedback from people they interact with in the organization. That will tell you much more than what an individual says about themselves.

Those who excel in their jobs are consistently achieving or exceeding their goals (relative to others) and constantly striving for higher goals. Many may not even celebrate their successes since they realize they can do better. Previously number-one women's singles tennis player Naomi Osaka said this after her loss at the 2021 US Open: "I feel like for me recently, when I win I don't feel happy. I feel more like a relief. And then when I lose, I feel very sad. I don't think that's normal."[9] People who are good have much higher expectations for themselves. For them, there is always another level of achievement to reach, another level of excellence to strive for. This is where a manager and an employee's peers need to ensure that the employee is encouraged and appreciated.

The key takeaway here is that leaders and managers must keep a finger on the pulse of the organization to identify the skills and the traits for each individual and help identify what that individual is good at. A good manager will be able to identify an employee's strengths from some of the behaviors described and use that to guide their approach to work management for that individual.

As a manager, if you had judged Naomi Osaka's skill and performance as a swimmer, you would been very disappointed, and Naomi would have probably quit. A famous quote that is misattributed to Einstein but still rings true is: "Everyone is a genius. But if you judge a fish by its ability to climb a tree, it will live its whole life believing that it is stupid."

Managers must then align that individual with roles and activities that harness their strengths. It is also important to consider providing continuous challenges and learning opportunities so the individual can continue to grow, excel, and improve their skills. In one of the major surveys conducted during the "Great Resignation" by Pew Research, lack of opportunities for growth was cited as the second biggest reason for leaving an organization.[10]

HARNESSING THAT SKILL

An issue that organizations may have to deal with is people who are really good at something eventually either burning out or growing out of enjoying their work. This will land them in either purple zone 3 or red zone 2. This was the case with Naomi Osaka, who eventually decided to take an extended break from tennis. The best managers and organizational leaders need to know who their Naomi Osakas are in their field of work and nurture them for long-term performance and to avoid burnout in their roles.

It then becomes clear that organizational leaders and managers must always be aware of this and make extra efforts to ensure and identify key areas that the individual is good at and then do the following.

ALIGN MORE WORK TO THEIR STRENGTHS

Drew Fortin, CEO of Lever Talent, an expert in talent strategy, says, "We are too often pigeonholed into roles because that's what our management demands of us, or we are driven by other factors (like compensation) without the opportunity to articulate our desire or discover our superpowers. Counter to what many believe, you will get better results focusing on developing things you are already strong at versus trying to correct areas where you are not so talented."[11]

Once you have identified an individual's strengths, it's time to identify those areas of work in your organization or teams where their skills can be put to good and beneficial use. Identify the needed skills in your functional group that most match with the individual's strengths. There is almost never a perfect fit, as not all the skills required in that role may align with the employee's strengths. But that's OK, as long as there is a deliberate and intentional approach, and the organization is cognizant of what the employee does and doesn't do well. It must be noted that sometimes a better skill-profile match may happen to be in other areas in your organization. An organization must be diligent in finding the best fit for an employee utilizing their overall skills. It is critical not to be a talent hoarder as this may backfire for your team either internally or externally based on where the strengths align.

GIVE CONSTRUCTIVE FEEDBACK AND SHOW APPRECIATION FOR THEIR WORK

People who are good at what they do are generally looking to improve their skills. An organization should develop an open feedback system with them so that they can get constructive feedback regarding areas in which they can improve. However, it is important to ensure this feedback is meaningful and outcome focused, not just feedback for feedback's sake. Some of this feedback can come from a well-designed 360 feedback process.

GIVE THEM TOOLS AND RESOURCES TO GET BETTER

An employee who is good at a skill but doesn't have the right tools or resources at their disposal will end up underutilized and not fully realizing their potential. An organization should double down on the areas of their strengths but provide the individual with the tools and resources that they can use to improve and excel to bring better outcomes in their role.

The individual should be set up for challenging work in that area, so they continue to learn and grow. People who are good at something seldom sit around basking in their laurels; they want to continue to learn, improve, and grow their skills. A manager should work with that employee to set up challenging work that helps them get better at their skills, which will lead to better outcomes at their job. The manager should also strive to ensure that these challenges are attainable and realistic while also making sure they are aligned with a larger purpose within the organization.

There is an important distinction between being really good at something and simply enjoying it. As we discussed in this chapter, an individual may be good at a certain skill as seen by some of the traits they display, but sometimes they just really enjoy their work area but are not that good at it. If the individual is self-aware of their abilities, they may know that they are not good at this skill, but many times that is not the case. The manager's role then becomes understanding this distinction and acting accordingly.

KEY TAKEAWAYS

- Skill development is the result of passion, hard work, and repetition, rather than innate talent alone. Genetics and environmental factors can play a role, but dedication and practice are essential for mastery.

- Environment, including supportive parents or leadership, coaches, and dedicated time, is crucial for achieving world-class success. The quality of practice and motivation also matter.

- Assessing someone's proficiency in a skill or job can be challenging. The Dunning–Kruger Effect highlights the tendency for people to overestimate their abilities, particularly in areas where they lack expertise. Objective benchmarks, 360-degree feedback, and recognizing signs of proficiency, such as seeking feedback, exceeding goals, and helping peers, can also indicate competence.

- It's essential for managers to align individuals with roles that leverage their strengths and provide opportunities for growth. Feedback, resources, and challenging tasks should be tailored to help individuals continue to excel and improve their skills.

- Understanding the difference between being good at something and simply enjoying it is crucial. Not everyone who enjoys a task is necessarily skilled at it, and managers should recognize this distinction when assessing an individual's abilities and preferences.

3

WHAT THE PERSON IS PASSIONATE ABOUT

Find a job you enjoy doing, and you will never have to work a day in your life.

The provenance of that saying is murky and has been credited to many people over the centuries, from Confucius to Mark Twain, and many other people respected for their intellect and insight. But the truth is actually much more complicated than that. You cannot find what you love until you explore a variety of jobs and activities. You might think you love doing something until you get the opportunity to do it professionally, and then reality sets in and you learn it is not the dream job you imagined it to be. And that is only if the opportunity presents itself in the first place. Typically, you fall into a job because it was the first one available to you, or the one that offered you the highest income at that time. As time passes, you become good at it, and it starts paying you more, and it becomes almost too easy not to continue doing the same job day in and day out.

But can you become passionate about that job? It really depends on how you look at it. Some aspects of any given job may be very interesting to an individual, especially if you are learning and growing in the job. Other activities may seem like drudgery and probably something you have to force yourself to do as part of the job. Research shows that passion is not a limited set that is predetermined at birth but one that can be cultivated.[1]

In the paper "Implicit Theories of Interest: Finding Your Passion or Developing It?" the authors find that "if interests are developed, then having a strong interest in one area does not preclude developing interests elsewhere. Moreover, the belief that interests are developed, not revealed fully formed, implies that this development may sometimes be difficult. If so, a growth theory of interest may help sustain interest in the face of frustration or difficulty."[2]

Before I delve into talking about the role passion plays at work, it is important to explore what passion is. An often-repeated phrase and advice given to a lot of young people is to "follow your passion." However, there are several questions that arise from that:

- Do I even know my passion?

- Can my passion change as I get older?

- What if there is no commercial value to my passion? Do I live a life of penury and misery?

- Can I make something my passion even if I don't necessarily have an innate passion for it?

While "follow your passion" sounds well intentioned and fairly uncontroversial, it can actually lead you down a path of discontent, with suboptimal results. People are told to follow their passion in order to achieve success in their careers; however, this is not always the best advice, and success is not always attained. Even if there is some degree of success, it might not be enough to sustain a living on.

Passion is a powerful force, but it can also be blinding. When you're so passionate about something, it's easy to lose sight of the big picture and become single-mindedly focused on one thing. This can lead to tunnel vision and stagnation. Most people believe that in order to be successful, they need to find a job that they are passionate about. Though we would all like to have fun at our jobs, this criteria for one's career is not always practical or sustainable—or realistic.

Wendy Hamilton suggests a few approaches where she says, "There are a few ways to develop passion. The company's mission or purpose: If you feel the company is making an impact that you value on the world, then you can identify with it regardless of your role. The professional development you are receiving: If you feel you are growing as a human being—building a talent, skill, or getting better at living a value—then you can appreciate coming to work at a higher level. The motivation to serve/impact to others: If you value helping your external or 'internal customer coworkers,' then you can take pride in what you do and grow your drive."[3]

The author Michelle French-Holloway, in her book *A New Meaning–Mission Fit*, states that although the advice of finding your passion is well intentioned, it is somewhat misguided. She goes on to state that it's also about finding your strengths.[4]

There are other schools of thought on passion, one being that we are born with a predefined affinity for an activity, which sometimes can be attributed as *fixed mindset*. Another is that we can cultivate passion for a particular line of work. I would argue that, in our modern society, many activities were invented that would have been completely alien to our ancestors. Take, for example, a passion for artificial intelligence or cinematography.

Some people discover passion early in life, like how Tiger Woods started taking interest in golf at six months old after seeing his father play golf. By the time he was five years old, he was featured in *Golf Digest* magazine. Compare that to the great cricket legend Sachin Tendulkar, who was passionate about tennis and imitated John McEnroe while very young. However, his elder brother enrolled him in a cricket academy at the age of ten, and his passion shifted to that sport, leading to his debut in international cricket at the age of sixteen, making him the youngest person to play a sport internationally. Passion can be inherent, as in the case of Tiger Woods, or it can be realized at a later stage after getting more exposure.

Passion can also be cultivated in such a way that you are not stuck with a passion from childhood. As a young teenager growing up in New Delhi, India, I was fascinated by rockets and space. I wanted to be a NASA scientist, working to ultimately launch the USS *Enterprise* in the future. While I had a lot of passion for the subject and for space, reality collided with my dreams and revealed that my skills in college, unfortunately, were not good enough to be a top scientist. With that dream extinguished, I developed a passion for technology entrepreneurship later in life and, even later still, I also developed a passion for making movies and music, which I pursue to this day.

There are also times in which you can rediscover your passion. One of the most impressive stories of developing passion or redeveloping passion later in life is the legend of Fauja Singh, a British citizen born in India in 1911.[5] He developed a passion for running at a young age, but he eventually gave it up and had a successful life and a family. After the death of his wife and son, and at the ripe age of eighty-nine, he returned to the passion of running. Years passed, and he participated in a marathon, which led to him currently holding the record for running a marathon at the age of one hundred. Passion that can be lost also can be regained, as Fauja Singh displayed.

The essence of these stories is that passion is not a fixed thing. Sometimes it is truly a passion that you gravitated toward at a young age, as in the case with Tiger Woods, or developed later in life, as in the case with Sachin Tendulkar, or rediscovered much later in life, as in the case of Fauja Singh.

In fact, it is possible to cultivate passion for your work, your craft. The skill growth you will experience from having a passion for your work will be fulfilling. There are several approaches one can take to reignite passion in your work or find a new line of work at your workplace or outside.

Drew Fortin says, "You need to connect your work to a higher purpose or value creation for the company. The statement that QC or accounting don't typically have passion is bogus. These individuals have an appreciation for structure, details, and processes. The QC employee is typically the last line of defense to ensure clients have the best product experience possible. The accounting employee has a passion for keeping accounts accurate. This is critical to the ongoing performance and runway the company has. Any perception that these employees are not passionate is a failure of their management to connect their team's charter to the company's broad mission, vision, and values."[6]

If you don't find passion in your work, it could be that you are bored of the work, or you are simply not good at it. One way to develop passion for your work is to make it a little more challenging and innovative. Sometimes it requires you to take a step back and reflect on why you chose this work in the first place. The work is still the same work you initially chose, and you might still choose it, but it is no longer as exciting as it was a few years ago. It may be time to take a time-out. Reflect on the goal you were working toward in that line of work, then come back with a renewed purpose and a different approach.

I once had an employee who was working in marketing, and it was clear from my interactions with her that she was not finding passion in her work. However, marketing was still her chosen calling. We worked together to discover what she cared about. She was passionate about helping people who were not given the right opportunities or were looked over in career progression, like women of color or people with different sexual identities. We worked on changing certain areas of her work so that she could focus on driving marketing messages to DEI (diversity, equity, and inclusion) activities and partner with organizations so that she could find meaning in her work.

When you have an employee who is passionate about a certain subject, it is important to give that passion some time to cultivate and lead to growth in their knowledge and experience. Time and action are the best predictors of whether that passion is real or not. When there is true passion, that individual will seek work on projects or activities in that area. On the other hand, if an individual is merely expressing their interest but not taking any real concrete action toward participating in the activities necessary for that passion to become a useful skill—the desire circle—then it's merely words and not true passion.

In the case of true passion, I often see an individual connecting with other people who they consider a coach or mentor who they can learn from. This coach or mentor can be internal or external to the organization. Many times, you will notice the person to be so passionate about that subject that they will come to you and request more projects or ideas in that area or devote more time working on these areas after normal work hours or on weekends.

It is important for a leader or manager to recognize this behavior in their people so as to better understand where true passion lies. As human beings, we all have blind spots, and we can lack self-awareness. If an employee expresses an interest in a role, but you can clearly see their passion lies in something else, it is important that you, as their leader, have a discussion with them about it.

As a manager, you have to get the best out of your people, and this often entails helping them find meaning in their work. Ask them a few questions like these:

- Why did you choose your current role in the first place?

- What skills do you have that you bring into this work and that you want to continue to improve upon?

- What are the areas of work in your current role that you absolutely despise doing?

- What would you rather be doing, at least some of the time at work, that the organization would find valuable?

- How can I, as a manager, help you?

Most managers are scared to ask these questions for fear of the answers. But having this important discussion is a first step toward finding alignment so that you get the best out of the people you are working with and so that they feel a sense of purpose.

Because of the systems many organizations are built upon, an employee may express interest in a role or activity only because it comes with broader responsibilities, exposure, and some prestige. And of course, they might be expressing an interest because it comes with higher pay. Many organizations mistake these elements for desire, when it is really about a perception of desire.

Organizations will often promote a high individual performer to a managerial role simply because they are afraid of losing them when they ask about their career role and express an interest in becoming a manager. Studies have shown that being a strong performer does not always lead to being a great manager, and, in fact, can have a negative effect on the overall organizational performance. An organization needs to be aware that managing a team is now no longer about an individual's performance but rather about getting the best from the team the individual manages. The same concept applies to other areas a person may express a desire for. For example, someone who works in the produce section of a grocery store may express a desire to work in the bakery department because they love cakes. But this desire alone doesn't qualify them. An employee's love of cakes may actually mean they just love eating a good cake, but that does not mean they can make one or even enjoy making one once they get into the nitty-gritty of baking a good cake. And even if they can bake cakes, they might not be that good at it.

It's also important to realize that people are not monoliths. We can have multiple interests and areas of work that we may enjoy. Someone may really enjoy analytical work and desire to work on market research, and also enjoy working on talent analytics, for example, or financial analysis. A manager's role then becomes opening up the cone of possibilities that better align a person's desires and skills with organizational needs. Assuming you realize the person is truly passionate about a certain subject or an activity, it can be a harmonious relationship to have activities aligned to those areas. When people work in the areas they truly enjoy, there is a positive correlation between that and engagement.

When engaged employees find their work more enjoyable, they turn that enjoyment into more effective action; work engagement is predicted by enjoyment but not by drive, the more typical "workaholism" component.[7]

If both the manager and employee are aligned on what the employee truly loves working on and is excited about, then the question turns to this:

IS THE INDIVIDUAL GOOD AT OR DO THEY SHOW ENOUGH COMPETENCY TO GET GOOD AT THESE ACTIVITIES?

Everyone has blind spots. Some blind spots are minor, and some are so big you could drive an 18-wheeler through them. Oftentimes, people will claim they are good at something but not realize that what they are actually saying is they *want* to be good at something, but they are not good at it yet. This is especially true when they see an expert do a task so flawlessly and fluidly that they come to believe they can do it too. In experiments published in *Psychological Science*, studies showed that people felt they can easily do something after they watched experts do it.[8] For example, watching a street performer flawlessly moonwalk does not mean you can do it too. The expert makes it look easy due to the hundreds or thousands of hours spent doing the task or activity. You may even be more inclined to think you can easily accomplish a task if you see it on YouTube. This can create a big blind spot.

For example, someone who is highly analytical and shows enough enthusiasm to work on projects related to market research will get good at this fairly quickly, even if they don't have the background yet. On the other hand, someone who is highly creative and highly social, but with little penchant for data, may struggle to get good at market research.

In this situation, it then becomes incumbent upon the manager to pursue the difference between fiction and possibility, perception and reality. It is incumbent for a good manager to develop the skill to be able to tell the difference between what is possible and what is a pipe dream for the employee.

As a manager, you want to always believe what the employee tells you they can be good at. However, for the benefit of the manager, the employee, and the organization, that claim must be grounded in reality. Ask yourself whether the employee has displayed glimpses of the skill in the past. Do they have an adjacent skill that can increase confidence of proficiency? Have they displayed enough believability based on both their words and actions in the past?

Edie Goldberg, PhD, an expert in talent management and the future of work, says, "Observe how they work (both alone and with others). When they are good at something, they are more productive and more creative. They lead, rather than follow."[9]

One mechanism to determine the employee's skill in an area is to assign activities that progressively increase the skill level required to perform them. This might need to be coupled with some coaching and training to help the employee learn and grow. The new models in modern management ask for the manager to act as a coach who helps their employee progress through active skill development. It will become apparent after a few turns whether the employee is progressing in that skill development and getting better at their role.

Here is an example of such a step-by-step approach for a person moving from the role of sales appointment setter, or BDR (business development representative)—basically someone who cold-calls or knocks on doors to set up appointments for the senior sales executive, who then will hopefully convert them to a client. A BDR's path to becoming a sales executive in a few months or a year might look like this:

- Learn as much as you can about the product or the service you are representing.

- Learn as much as you can about the ideal customer profile, the market, the competition.

- Tag along with a senior sales executive who is proficient at their job.

- Do a post-meeting assessment with the sales executive on why the customer purchased or did not purchase.

- Take relevant sales training pertinent to this role.

- Do a low-risk pitch accompanied by the sales executive and get post-pitch feedback.

- Continue taking on bigger prospects as you get better and move toward promotion.

The BDR would do this while in their current role, carving out time for the upskilling function.

Clearly, the BDR alone, without the necessary support from the organization, would not have sufficient skill to execute on this plan. The infrastructure and support the organization needs to provide includes competent sales executives who are interested in coaching others, allowing the BDR to set aside time for upskilling activities, and funding the right training, among other things. The organization's culture and strategy around employee development will be paramount here for this to succeed.

Furthermore, there are assessments such as CliftonStrengths and the Predictive Index Behavioral Assessment, among others, that organizations can have their people take that will help find their areas of strength and interest, including their working style. These can be very valuable in identifying the areas that the manager and the employee can work on together.

ARE THERE ENOUGH OF THESE ACTIVITIES TO KEEP THE EMPLOYEE ENGAGED?

There may be some areas where the employee can work that align well with their desires and also utilize their skills, but those pockets of activities may be far and few between. This can lead to frustration because the employee might have to then go back to doing activities that they may not enjoy the majority of the time. This can be a problem, and a longer-term solution to this must be mutually agreed upon with the employee and the manager. Oftentimes, this happens if the employee has been in the current role for a very long time or if the person was the wrong hire for that particular role to begin with. There are several ways to address this, but ultimately the solution will vary depending on the situation.

In my experience, when there is not enough work in the area that the employee wants to work on, it is best to work on a transition plan to help the employee move to an area within the company that better aligns with their desires, or even outside the organization where they may find more fulfillment.

Ultimately, if the employee can do a significant portion of their work in the areas of their interest, then the employee can be in the state of flow, which leads to job satisfaction and to high levels of overall performance and retention, as well as to being a more productive employee for the organization.

KEY TAKEAWAYS

- Passion for a particular job or activity is not something you're necessarily born with; it can be developed or discovered over time. People may have multiple interests, and their passions can evolve as they gain exposure to different experiences.

- The role of a manager or leader is helping employees align their passions with their skills and the organization's needs. This requires assessing an individual's capabilities and interests and finding ways to incorporate them into their current role or helping them transition to a more suitable one within or outside the organization.

- To ensure that an employee's passion aligns with their skills, managers can implement a step-by-step approach to continuous skill development. This may involve gradually increasing the complexity of tasks related to the desired area of passion while providing coaching and training as needed. It's important for managers to assess progress and competence objectively and not solely rely on an employee's self-assessment.

$$\frac{4}{}$$

WHAT THE ORGANIZATION VALUES AND NEEDS

*Individual commitment to a group effort—that is what makes
a team work, a company work, a society work, a civilization work.*

—Vince Lombardi

Broadly speaking, organizations establish a stated mission or purpose that serves as a long-term vision—a guiding light that unifies and aligns the team. This mission statement provides a clear direction and serves as a rallying point for the organization's activities. For instance, Walmart states its mission on their website: "We aim to build a better world—helping people live better and renew the planet while building thriving, resilient communities. For us, this means working to create opportunity, build a more sustainable future, advance diversity, equity and inclusion and bring communities closer together."[1] Similarly, United Way, a nonprofit organization, expresses its mission as: "United Way seeks to improve lives by mobilizing the caring power of communities around the world to advance the common good."[2] Likewise, the mission for the Government of Canada is stated as: "To promote and safeguard a non-partisan, merit-based and representative public service that serves all Canadians."[3] Although these missions may translate into varied activities across different business units, departments, and teams within an organization, the ultimate objective remains the same; each individual within the organization can regularly evaluate whether their work aligns with and contributes to the overarching mission, which serves as a guidepost for their actions.

The mission statement serves as a constant reminder of the organization's purpose and provides a framework for decision-making and prioritization. By ensuring alignment with the mission, organizations can work collectively toward achieving their long-term vision and making a meaningful impact on the world they serve.

DETERMINING VALUABLE SKILLS

Ian Ziskin, former CHRO of Northrup Grumman, now runs an HR strategy consulting firm. He says this of determining an employee's skills: "The quality of the person and their work is much more dependent on what they know and do than it is on their education and credentials. Most jobs can be deconstructed to better understand the skills required to perform the role effectively. The required skills—and how capable the person is to perform against those skill requirements—drive performance, results, and engagement."[4]

Let's use the example of a hypothetical marketing team in a for-profit technology organization. In this context, the organization highly values several key aspects from the marketing team, recognizing their critical role in driving business growth in the following areas:

- Brand awareness to the target customer

- Messaging to offer differentiation

- Activities to generate buyer interest

- Driving prospect leads to the sales funnel

There are more ways in which a mature marketing organization supports the growth and success of the overall organization. In addition to the previously mentioned aspects, the marketing organization places high value on various skills and activities that contribute to achieving their goals.

If we were to break down the short list of marketing goals into a sample (though not exhaustive) set of activities and skills, the following aspects would be considered essential:

Marketing Goals	Activities	Skills
Brand Awareness	• Develop digital ad campaigns • Sponsor events • Conduct educational seminars	• Copyediting skills • Graphic design skills • Presentation skills • Video editing skills • Marketing data analytic skills
Messaging to Offer Differentiation	• Create one-pagers • Create short videos • Gather customer testimonials and case studies	• Long form copywriting skills • Script writing skills • Interviewing skills • Research skills
Activities to Generate Buyer Interest	• Sign-ups for webinars • Conduct buyer conferences • Paid ads • Prospect segmentation	• Market research • Recruitment skills for speakers • Project management and organization skills • Analytic skills
Drive Prospect Leads to Sales Funnel	• Email campaigns • Building workflow cadences • Offering prospect incentives	• Workflow design • Email copywriting • Analytics and A/B testing

A seasoned marketing leader would then be able to put together a comprehensive chart, like the preceding one, that encompasses all their activities, mapping them to their goals. This valuable exercise would provide them with a comprehensive inventory of the skills available within the organization they manage.

So, a job in this marketing organization is essentially a collection of activities and skills that the organization values and is willing to compensate for. The crucial aspect then becomes the process of finding the right individuals who possess the required skills to perform these activities. However, as discussed earlier, employees may have an interest in these skills and activities but lack the proficiency to succeed in them. Conversely, they may possess the proficiency in these skills but lack the desire to engage in these activities.

The ideal scenario arises when an individual not only has the required skill proficiency but is also highly motivated to perform the activities, finding them fulfilling and enjoyable. This perfect alignment places them squarely in the blue zone of optimal performance. However, it is uncommon for one individual to possess the ideal combination of skills and motivation for every activity within a role.

As the preceding table illustrates, different activities within a brand awareness role can vary significantly, requiring diverse skill sets. Copyediting for brand awareness, for instance, demands different skills than market data analytics. This presents a challenge in identifying individuals who are both interested and motivated to perform the role, while also possessing the requisite skills in each area to achieve success.

Addressing this challenge involves a strategic approach to talent acquisition and management, such as building cross-functional teams or developing career paths that allow individuals to specialize in specific areas while collaborating with others to cover the broader range of activities. By recognizing the diversity of skills and activities within a role and implementing strategies to harness collective expertise, organizations can maximize their chances of finding individuals who are not only proficient but also motivated to contribute effectively to the overall objectives.

It then becomes imperative for the marketing leader to clearly define the activities and skills that hold significant value for the organization in driving the mission forward and achieving the overall objectives.

In doing so, they can effectively prioritize the activities and skills that are of utmost importance for the team members to possess. In cases where some skills may require upskilling, you can then focus on that development.

It is crucial to acknowledge that organizations, regardless of their size and funding, do not possess infinite resources. In fact, I have yet to encounter an organization that has all the desired resources and skills at its disposal. Therefore, it becomes paramount for the leaders of each function within the organization to accurately prioritize the activities and the associated skills required to ensure maximum impact.

By strategically focusing on the most crucial activities and homing in on the essential skills, leaders can optimize resource allocation and enhance the team's ability to deliver results. This entails making thoughtful decisions regarding which activities and skills should take precedence and allocating resources accordingly. Through this careful prioritization, your organization can effectively navigate resource limitations and drive success in alignment with your mission.

I presented the small exercise in the preceding table for a marketing organization, which, by any measure, is merely a glimpse of the comprehensive approach required. However, it serves as an illustration of the approach that every organization, suborganization, and function can undertake. The aim is to break down goals into a detailed set of activities and the corresponding skills needed to achieve those goals.

Subsequently, the crucial step is to prioritize these goals, activities, and skills, considering the potential impact relative to the effort invested.

By undertaking this process, each team can define their unique organizational values circle, aligning their activities and skills with the broader organizational objectives. This allows for a deliberate focus on the key elements that will have the most significant impact on achieving the desired outcomes. The process is not only about identifying and prioritizing goals but also about establishing a clear understanding of the activities and skills that contribute to organizational success.

While the preceding exercise is far from comprehensive, it demonstrates the starting point for organizations to embark on a systematic analysis of their goals, activities, and skills. By following this approach, you can gain valuable insights into your company's unique requirements, enabling you to allocate resources effectively and achieve maximum impact in line with your strategic objectives.

SKILLS-BASED ORGANIZATION

There is a notable trend toward establishing a skills-based organization, wherein traditional roles become more fluid. In this context, a singular role like brand awareness, as exemplified in the preceding scenario, may not be carried out by a single individual. Instead, it would be deconstructed into a collection of skills and performed by different individuals, depending on their respective interests and proficiency levels.

This evolving approach signifies that individuals can assume roles that are inherently flexible and span across multiple teams within the organization. It introduces a concept akin to being a free agent within the organization, where individuals can leverage their diverse skill sets to contribute to different teams. For instance, an engineer possessing proficient graphic design skills and a passion for teaching could fulfill a fluid role. They might allocate a substantial portion of their time to coding and software development, while also dedicating some of their time to crafting visually appealing presentations for junior developers. Moreover, they could serve as a brand ambassador for the company, sharing their expertise on various platforms and speaking at conferences.

This model of fluid roles and cross-functional contributions allows individuals to maximize the utility of their skills and adapt to varying team needs. By embracing this approach, organizations can tap into the vast range of talents their employees possess, promoting versatility, collaboration, and knowledge sharing across different domains.

The future of work within every organization is undoubtedly heading toward a significant emphasis on skills-based work. As this transition unfolds, traditional roles and job titles will likely become more fluid and adaptable. This shift presents enhanced opportunities for aligning what the organization values with the diverse skill sets that employees can offer across various aspects of the value chain. Consequently, employees will no longer be confined to a singular group or department, enabling them to explore and contribute to different areas within the organization, breaking free from limitations that previously hindered their mobility and growth. This evolution promises a more dynamic and agile work environment, fostering increased collaboration, innovation, and the optimal utilization of talent throughout the organization's operations.

Increasingly, many progressive organizations are moving to this skills-based approach in to their organizational construct. This requires an organization to take a completely different approach to hiring and managing careers within the organization—a skills-based organization has the potential to place a larger number of individuals in the coveted blue zone of optimal performance.

Edie Goldberg, coauthor of the book *The Inside Gig*, says this about building a skills-based organization: "Employees want to learn and grow.

In fact, recent research indicates career growth is more important than pay for most employees. When the organization understands *all* of the skills an employee has, as well as the skills they want to develop, they can connect employees with both job-based opportunities and projects that provide the right amount of stretch to keep them learning and growing, as well as building the skills important for the future of the company."[5]

A skills-based organization focuses on matching people to tasks, activities, and projects based on the skills they have or the skills they want to develop, as opposed to job titles they are given. This is a major shift, which requires organizations to think of a job's role as a collection of skills rather than just a job title that assumes a monolithic approach to a person in that role. This stands in contrast to the limitations of conventional approaches relying on rigidly defined roles and responsibilities, paving the way for a more agile and dynamic workforce that maximizes individual potential and contributes to overall organizational success.

In an article for *Deloitte Insights*, Cantrell et al. (2020) define skills as technical abilities, such as coding or accounting, and cognitive abilities, such as critical thinking and emotional intelligence, and they include potential skills that could be developed in the future.[6] Focusing on these aspects of work ability is good not just for the employee but also for the organization. According to the same research study, organizations that adopt a skills-based approach are 98 percent more likely to retain high performers.[7]

This strategic approach to skills-based work can greatly optimize the utilization of human capital resources within the organization. It acknowledges the reality that no organization, whether for profit, nonprofit, or governmental, possesses all the desired resources, particularly the required skills, within a single resource. By deconstructing jobs into the specific skills needed and allowing fluidity within the organization, managers can avoid the trap of talent hoarding within their teams.

This shift in mindset ensures that valuable skills are not confined to specific individuals or teams but are instead shared and leveraged across the organization. It breaks down barriers and encourages collaboration and knowledge exchange, enabling a more efficient allocation of resources based on the specific skills required for each task or project.

Embracing this approach not only enhances the overall effectiveness and productivity of the workforce but also fosters an environment of continuous learning and growth. It enables the organization to tap into the full spectrum of skills and expertise available, leading to innovation, agility, and adaptability.

By dismantling traditional job structures and embracing the fluidity of skills within the organization, talent can be more effectively mobilized, resources can be optimized, and the organization can achieve higher levels of performance and success.

EVOLVING SKILLS FOR A VUCA WORLD

Today we live in a world dominated by VUCA—volatility, uncertainty, complexity, ambiguity—a leadership theory that proposes that things are always changing fast, and you never know what's coming next, especially in certain businesses.[8] To deal with it, we have to stop using old ways of doing things and learn to be flexible every day. In this VUCA world we currently inhabit, change is not only inevitable but is actually accelerating. When we examine the span of the last three years, starting from early 2020 and extending to the end of 2022, the magnitude of fluctuations and shifts in organizational needs propelled by social and economic uncertainties has rapidly intensified. This acceleration has reached a point where if we were to reflect on it a decade ago or so, such rapid and profound changes would have been beyond imagination. Consequently, organizations are now compelled to adopt an agile approach to business and adapt to the evolving skill requirements within their workforce. Remarkably, many of the skills demanded today didn't even exist a mere few years ago, underscoring the dynamic and ever-evolving nature of the modern business landscape.

Given the constantly evolving and ever-changing environment in which we operate, the list of skills that your organization values will always remain in a state of flux. What was highly valued and sought after just a few years ago may no longer hold the same significance. However, your team may have adjacent skills that can be shifted to fit your new need. It may take some retraining, some of your team members may need to change projects or teams, and, in the most drastic cases, they may not fit your needs anymore.

For instance, reflecting on my own career as a software developer in the mid-1990s with a prominent US mainframe computer company, the most coveted skill at the time was COBOL, a computer programming language. However, its relevance began to wane as Microsoft's Visual Basic and Borland's PowerBuilder gained momentum. Borland's PowerBuilder and another front-end software called Delphi enjoyed a period of popularity due to their exceptional capabilities. However, within a couple of years, Microsoft's marketing and sales efforts dominated the market with Visual Basic, and subsequently Visual C++. As a result, despite PowerBuilder being, in my opinion, a superior development platform, it gradually lost its relevance as fewer organizations required it.

This example serves as a reminder of how rapidly the landscape can shift and how organizations must continually adapt to changing skill demands. It highlights the importance of staying attuned to emerging technologies and evolving trends, ensuring that the skill sets within your organization align with the current and future needs of the industry. By remaining agile and proactive in identifying and acquiring relevant skills, organizations can stay ahead of the curve and maintain their competitive edge in an ever-evolving business environment.

Amid these changes, though, there was a silver lining. It was discovered that the required skills for PowerBuilder and Microsoft's Visual Basic were closely related. As a result, individuals could smoothly transition from one skill to the other in a remarkably short period of time, typically a few days. This realization brought about a sense of hope and provided a favorable outlook amid the evolving landscape.

More recently, in the past few years, a notable shift occurred when Figma gained prominence, bringing about a significant demand for Figma skills within design teams. However, it became apparent that the pool of individuals possessing expertise in Figma was relatively limited. Yet, upon closer examination, it became evident that individuals well-versed in Adobe Photoshop or Illustrator possessed a strong foundation, which facilitated a smooth transition to utilizing Figma. The similarities and shared principles between these tools allowed for an easy adaptation and quick mastery of Figma's features and capabilities.

As organizations determine the skills necessary for their success, it becomes imperative for them to not only assess the existing skill sets within their workforce, but also to explore the area of adjacent skills that can be adapted to the ever-accelerating changes in technology and tools. This dynamic landscape is witnessing the birth of new skill requirements while simultaneously witnessing the retirement of older ones. It is essential to acknowledge that no single individual can possess all the skills needed to excel in any given role.

FLUID WORK IN A SKILLS-BASED ORGANIZATION

To navigate this ever-changing landscape, it is necessary to not only redefine but also reconstruct the very nature of roles themselves. Embracing this dynamic environment entails fostering adaptability and embracing fluidity in roles, allowing for fractional staffing approaches tailored to specific projects. For a more in-depth discussion of this topic, I highly recommend authors Ravin Jesuthasan and John Boudreau's illuminating book *Work without Jobs*, which provides keen insights and thought-provoking perspectives.[9]

As technology continues to advance with the integration of artificial intelligence and machine learning in the realm of workforce management, organizations gain the ability to swiftly and effectively prioritize, de-prioritize, and re-prioritize their skill requirements for various initiatives and projects. With the emergence of cutting-edge platforms like Engagedly, a people strategy and management software company that I lead, organizations are witnessing a rapid evolution in the form of comprehensive talent intelligence systems. These platforms offer invaluable and in-depth insights into the available talent pool's diverse skill sets, as well as the skills demanded by different initiatives within the organization. The leadership can leverage this wealth of information to gain crucial insights into skill gaps, identify the upward and downward trends of specific skills, and consequently enhance their workforce planning and employee development programs. This strategic approach facilitates better decision-making and empowers organizations to optimize their human capital for sustainable growth and success.

At Engagedly, this is one of the core tenets we started adopting a few years ago. As a start-up, we couldn't afford to hire a specialist for every role, and, in fact, it may not even be advisable to do so during a company's beginning since the roles are rapidly evolving. When we realized we really couldn't afford to do that, we started adopting a skills-based approach where one individual in a different function could pitch in on a short project that was a different from their current role.

For example, we started having our product managers create and edit videos as marketing and sales collaterals. Traditionally, product managers would write a product brief and hand it over to marketing or sales to take to market. But we realized that was an ineffective and inefficient model. The best people to talk about the value of the product, the use cases, and the problems it addressed were the product managers. Creating marketing videos is not a skill set you see in job descriptions for product managers, but we made use of our unique employees' existing skills and built up those skills when we needed to. These were short projects outside of the realm of the product managers but clearly something they seemed to enjoy and do well. This ultimately helped the marketing teams as well as the sales teams better position our solutions to our customers.

The key takeaway to remember is that an organization's perception of valuable skills and competencies is a dynamic and ever-changing collection. Without incorporating agility into their human capital systems and processes, organizations will struggle to accurately identify the skills they truly require at any given time.

KEY TAKEAWAYS

- Mission statements serve as a long-term vision and guiding light for organizations. They provide a clear direction and rally the team around a common purpose.

- Skills are more important than education and credentials in determining a person's quality of work. Jobs can be deconstructed into specific skills required for effective performance.

- The concept of skills-based organizations is gaining prominence as roles become fluid, and tasks are performed by individuals with relevant skills and interests. This approach maximizes the utility of employees' skills, fosters collaboration, and promotes versatility.

YOUR CULTURE CIRCLE

I came to see, in my time at IBM, that culture isn't just one aspect of the game—it is the game. In the end, an organization is nothing more than the collective capacity of its people to create value.

—Louis Gerstner (former CEO of IBM)

The outermost circle of the workplace ikigai zones, the culture circle, encompasses the diagram's three circles by providing a supporting environment where movement from red or purple zones can be facilitated. This is a people-centric culture circle.

The Society for Human Resource Management (SHRM), a leading organization for HR practitioners, has a really good definition of culture:

An organization's culture is based on values derived from basic assumptions about the following:

Human nature: *Are people inherently good or bad, mutable or immutable, proactive or reactive? These basic assumptions lead to beliefs about how employees, customers, and suppliers should interact and how they should be managed.*

The organization's relationship to its environment: *How does the organization define its business and its constituencies?*

Appropriate emotions: *Which emotions should people be encouraged to express, and which ones should be suppressed?*

Effectiveness: *What metrics show whether the organization and its individual components are doing well? An organization will be effective only when the culture is supported by an appropriate business strategy and a structure that is appropriate for both the business and the desired culture.*[1]

Let's take these four attributes of an organization and see what they mean for the organization's culture.

Human Nature

If the organization treats humans as inherently good, then the organization is more focused on building a culture of trust and transparency. There is an inherent trust between people within the organization and across levels. However, if the organization sees people as inherently bad, then there is a culture of mistrust. There will be a lot of secret agendas within the teams and by the management. The teams will be working without a level of transparency and trust, leading to suboptimal outcomes and a lack of loyalty.

If the human nature assumptions focus on the immutability of humans, then the organization will lack a focus on employee growth and development. However, if the organization inherently believes that people are mutable and, as such, can grow into new roles by learning new skills, then there is a growth mindset at these organizations.

If the human nature at these organizations is more reactive, then the culture will always be looking at problems after they occur, and finger-pointing will be the norm of people within and between teams. A proactive human nature will drive for better planning and seeing problems before they manifest themselves, leading to an organizational culture that works together for solutions rather than fixing problems as or after they occur.

Relationship to the Environment

Who does the organization consider as its stakeholder? For far too long, many organizations—at least in our capitalist system—have made shareholders the primary stakeholder. This has led to a very profit-minded culture. In such a culture, people and customers become tools to achieve the highest profits possible. However, in an organization that has a more holistic approach to its environment, where the stakeholders are not only the investors but also their employees, their customers, and the larger society within which they operate, decisions are made that positively impact everyone, or at least the outcome is balanced among several different objectives beyond simple profit. This leads to a culture of empathy and a focus on employee growth, customers, initiatives that positively drive inclusion, and a better environment for the society.

Appropriate Emotions

Does the organization support differing points of view, or does it shut down voices that don't agree with their leadership and managers? Do people feel a psychological safety at their workplace to be themselves and express their ideas? Do they feel they can give and receive feedback without fear of retribution? If the organization does not provide an environment where people can express their emotions without being judged, then new ideas will be suppressed, and there will be a lack of innovation. The people will lack emotional investment in their work, and the culture will be built on mistrust, with a focus on self-preservation rather than teamwork.

A positive work culture encourages people to speak up when they disagree. Disagreement backed by evidence, or arguments for their viewpoint, must be actively encouraged so ideas are battle-tested. Organizations should build an ecosystem where management does not have the monopoly on ideas and opinions. If every idea managers or leaders come up with is treated as the new law of the land, with no mechanism for feedback from the employees who are on the frontlines, one will never be able to prevent bigger problems from negatively impacting the organization's performance. Bringing one's true self to work as an employee must be encouraged if the organization wants strong work outcomes.

Effectiveness

What gets measured gets managed. A lack of organizational metrics often leads to an organization that doesn't know how it's performing. People can't keep themselves and others accountable. The business strategy becomes mere words in a PowerPoint with no mechanism to implement and measure its effectiveness. The culture of such an organization will lack a mechanism to recognize and reward effectiveness or correct ineffectiveness within teams.

Organizations that set goals that are transparent to the rest of the teams allow the team members to then set their goals that align to the overall business objectives. These goals set by the team members need to be specific and measurable so that the team members can show measurable progress against them. This will not only keep them accountable, but it will also help them keep each other accountable. The transparency of the goals, measurement, and effectiveness will create a culture where waste can be identified and reduced.

A culture is not one attribute or a metric that can be posted on a wall; it is a complex set of attributes that defines how an organization views people within and outside the organization and drives how people interact with each other.

Wendy Hamilton has a great perspective on culture: "Corporations exist to make money, to make profit specifically. Values are what is even more important than making money, such that you'd sacrifice some money to achieve them. And then culture is how you action your values: how you make decisions, how you communicate, how you embed values into your day-to-day priorities."[2]

WHAT MAKES A COMPANY CULTURE GREAT?

Is it the happy hours on Friday or the pizza parties at lunch time? Or is it the management that shows true empathy and cares for its people? If we look at the true measures of a good culture, it embodies itself within how the people behave. It shows in the emotions people have when they go to bed on a Sunday night, knowing that Monday is coming. Does the employee dread their Monday mornings and their discussions with their organizational leaders on any given day? Do they feel comfortable speaking their mind? Do they feel respected within the organization? Since culture is a nebulous concept, it is hard to put a metric on what makes a great culture, but the results from employee sentiments, organizational performance, employee retention, etc., can shed light on the effectiveness of the organization's culture.

Ian Ziskin says this about great cultures: "There is no one culture that is right for everyone. What makes it great is that a particular employee base values it; it's part of the value proposition of their employment. A great culture to me means that employee would accept less pay than they could get elsewhere because the culture's value to them is great."[3]

Melissa Widner, CEO of financial services firm Lighter Capital, drives home that alignment to the mission is what makes for a great culture, emphasizing the importance of "passion for the mission, [a] collaborative work environment, the knowledge that team members care about each other."[4]

If you ask the leadership to rate their culture, every company will claim to embody a great culture. If only that were true. Some organizations define culture based on how their employees feel, while others define culture purely on business performance. While it is hard to see for many leaders, there is a direct correlation between how people feel at their workplace and how the organization performs, assuming all things remain the same.

We have all heard of company cultures that were a toxic cesspool because there was so much emphasis on the bottom line and the shareholder value. A famous, or rather notorious, example of a toxic company culture was Sunbeam in the '90s. Sunbeam was led by their unapologetically toxic CEO, nicknamed "Chainsaw Al." As the head of Scott Paper and later Sunbeam Corp., Al Dunlap was well known for his "bottom line at any cost" style of leadership. In his first weeks into his tenure, he fired over six thousand people—about half his workforce—and continued to make life miserable for the remaining employees. The stock price shot up by more than 50 percent.[5] This was a temporary blip in a long-term decline, which often happens when a toxic culture takes hold. In such an environment, a culture of innovation suffers, engagement levels sink, and eventually missionaries become mercenaries. Almost all of Sunbeam's US factories were shut down and moved overseas, leading to a loss of innovation. Sunbeam then announced in 1998 (twice in three weeks) that their revenue and profits would be well below Wall Street's expectations.

Eventually, Chainsaw Al was fired after being accused of accounting fraud in 1998. Later, Al Dunlap even had the audacity to translate his experiences of leading with toxic style into a book called *Mean Business: How I Save Bad Companies and Make Good Companies Great.*

Restatement of their financial statements lead to increased loss and inability to pay debts accrued from bad acquisitions; this, compounded by the decline in sales, ended up proving fatal for the company.

Al Dunlap believed he was building a great culture—a culture of accountability and ruthless focus on profits and shareholder value. Nothing could have been further from the truth. Back then we did not have employee voice tools that could amplify their issues with the culture in a public forum, like Glassdoor or LinkedIn, so very little is known about the real voice of the employees from the '90s.

When there are mass layoffs, people lose psychological safety. Management can get away with bad ideas, and even fraud. We don't have the actual voices of the Sunbeam employees, but we know that this approach assumed that people were disposable tools and mere numbers on a spreadsheet. Dunlap failed to define the business within its environment, because his entire approach was driven by a spreadsheet, and a bad one at that. We know that emotions in a culture of this sort are suppressed unless they feed the ego of the corrupt leader. And in the end, it was anything but effective.

We know now that great cultures are the ones where employees can thrive. This is where employees feel a sense of belonging and purpose to drive the organization forward toward its mission.

One of those organizations where culture matters is FedEx. When I was at FedEx, early in my career, they had a strong culture of supporting continuing education and employee development, which allowed me to take training and attend conferences that furthered my interests. The one thing FedEx did really well was employee recognition. They had a program called Bravo Zulu, among other awards, which was a spot award that a manager could give an employee at any time.[6] At that time, it was a $100 cash award (after tax), which was a lot for a twenty-something in the '90s. I ended up getting eight of those awards in a period of eighteen months. That was because it really motivated me to take on more responsibilities and stay longer to get things done. It was one of many things that drove a very employee-friendly culture at FedEx. They had one of the lowest employee turnover rates in the region and were frequently awarded many workplace culture awards.

In a great culture, an employee feels connected and is motivated. This allows for employees to work better together and drive higher levels of profitability and growth for the organization.

Burnout

The reason the culture circle is important in the ikigai model is that if the culture is not supportive to the employees, then, regardless of the type of work the employee is doing, which may very well be in the blue zone, the outcomes for both the employees and the organization are going to be suboptimal. As we will discuss later, identifying the areas of work and the zones employees are in and moving them to a blue zone of work requires intent from both the employee and the manager. If the culture is not supportive and is more focused on bottom-line results, the manager will be more focused on managing up and driving people in her team into the burnout zone instead of the blue zone. Research studies show that employee burnout was on the rise during the pandemic, which progressive organizations took note of and implemented several initiatives to improve the culture of remote work.[7]

Employee burnout is an organizational issue, not an employee issue.[8] Authors Michael Mankins and Eric Garton, in their book, *Time, Talent, Energy*, note that "when employees aren't as productive as they could be, it's usually the organization, not its employees, that is to blame. The same is true for employee burnout."[9]

A toxic culture will increase burnout. But even a good culture can cause burnout if the organization doesn't properly tend to it. There are high-performance cultures where people are highly engaged and collaborative. However, research shows that people in high-performance cultures can also get to a state of burnout because they don't know when to say no and set boundaries so they can rest and recuperate.

A good culture will take proactive action for employees to avoid burnout. For example, the leading music and podcast streaming service Spotify gave employees the week of October 31, 2022, off, as a wellness week.[10] This allowed employees to check out of their inbox and spend time with their family and friends or just relax.

A good culture is not a checklist of items, like a wellness week, foosball tables in the cafeteria, a declared open-door policy, etc., but an ecosystem that lives and breathes empathy and compassion while maintaining a high-performance mindset among its employees.

Burnout is not a necessary outcome of employees in an organization that is trying to get the best out of its people. When employees do their best work because they are doing work that fuels their purpose and makes them feel appreciated, they are less likely to experience burnout.

This is especially true when that work aligns with skills they are working to master. This work then becomes more like an athlete working to achieve their personal best. The organization becomes their audience, where they feel supported and even cheered. This can help the employee push through hard problems and deliver outcomes that align with the organizational strategy.

Cultural Responsibility

Many organizational leaders outsource culture to their HR department. Somehow, there is a belief in organizational magic in otherwise intelligent and wise leaders who run the organization. This magical belief that HR can wave a wand and the organization will have a great culture is not only not true but is actually dangerous for the overall culture at the organization. Too often, the organizational leader will pay lip service to building a great culture in their town halls, or in the emails they send out to the organization, while living in a different reality with their own teams. Effective leadership entails building a strong culture of empathy, accountability, and respect for all people in the organization, regardless of their title or function.

An effective culture permeates the entire organization. This implies that every leader, starting with the CEO, exhibits behaviors that set the example for the culture and drives other behaviors throughout the company. The CEO's behaviors are very powerful and drive the next rung of leader behaviors. This cascades throughout the organization.

For example, we have all emailed our colleagues or our managers and gotten no response for days. Then we will email them a reminder a few days later. This leads to frustration, lost energy and time, and ultimately impacts effective teamwork. However, if the CEO sets the behavior that all internal emails get answered, or at a minimum acknowledged, within one business day, that behavior will be adopted widely by others as well. I have seen firsthand where a culture of responsiveness or a culture of respect transcends throughout the organization because the leader leads by example. The opposite is also true. If there is lack of responsiveness or lack of respect where abusive behavior is tolerated or even exhibited by the leaders, the organizational culture will turn toxic and permeate the entire organization.

You could have a great manager and good peer group within your team, but if the organizational culture does not support good camaraderie, a focus on employee development and growth, openness to ideas from all corners of the organization (not just from the top management), and appreciation from their management, then it does not lend itself to an ikigai-friendly environment.

While within the team the employee and the manager may be aligned on the ikigai principles of working in the blue zone, it is important to find an alignment where a large portion of the activities performed are in the employee's zone of high desire and can demonstrate high levels of skill. And from the manager's perspective, these areas are extremely valuable to the organization. However, the organizational culture can make or break the blue zone if the employee doesn't feel connected to the organization and does not feel psychologically safe in that environment. This can result from a culture where risk-taking is frowned upon and employees are punished for failure rather than allowing that failure to serve as a learning opportunity. It may also result from a culture where speaking up or voicing dissenting ideas are discouraged by people at higher ranks. Leadership that encourages people to express themselves and challenge ideas, allowing the best ideas to win, and that encourages learning by allowing people to take on new challenges or roles where they may not be fully skilled yet will lead to a culture where blue zones will thrive and be found aplenty.

In the context of the alignment between work, the employee, and the manager, the organizational culture needs to be considered as the environment that sustains it. Don't give it enough oxygen and even the best alignments between employees and managers will fail.

There is no single right answer to what makes a great culture, as it varies by organization, industry, geography, and country culture. However, several tools can help measure and benchmark your organizational culture, like CultureIQ and Engagedly, which can help you better understand your organization's culture. This will help you determine whether your organization's culture is what you anticipated it to be or if there is a change required.

KEY TAKEAWAYS

- There are four key attributes that shape an organization's culture: human nature, its relationship to the environment, appropriate emotions, and effectiveness.

- A supportive culture is essential for employee well-being. Employee burnout is an organizational issue. Even high-performance cultures can contribute to burnout if boundaries and rest are not prioritized.

- Organizational leaders play a critical role in shaping culture by setting examples and behaviors that cascade throughout the company. Leadership behaviors determine building a culture of respect, responsiveness, and psychological safety, and how this culture affects employees' ability to find their ikigai (a sense of purpose).

6

FINDING THE BLUE ZONE

Striving to find meaning in one's life is the primary motivational force in man.

—Viktor Frankl

I n his book *Man's Search for Meaning*, Viktor Frankl argues that finding meaning and purpose in life is essential for human well-being.[1] It helps us find motivation to move forward and to endure difficult challenges in our lives. Frankl, an Austrian psychiatrist and Holocaust survivor, drew upon his experiences in Nazi concentration camps to explore the psychological and existential aspects of human suffering.

Frankl contended that individuals possess the freedom to choose their attitudes and responses to the challenges they face, regardless of their circumstances. He emphasized that while people cannot always control what happens to them, they can always choose how they react and find meaning in their lives.[2]

Frankl also introduced the concept of logotherapy, which is based on the belief that meaning can be discovered in three primary ways:

through engaging in meaningful work or creative endeavors, experiencing deep connections with others through love and relationships, and finding meaning in the face of suffering or unavoidable situations.[3]

According to Frankl, a sense of purpose and meaning can provide individuals with the strength and resilience to overcome adversity and find fulfillment, even amid challenges. This directly leads to improvement of their skills and competencies in that area as they become more focused.[4]

How does that translate for a workplace blue zone? For an employee to be in the blue zone, they need to find meaning and purpose in their work. This means they work with intent and are engaged in that work. This does not mean that the work is fun or delightful, by any means, but it has to have meaning that the employee can connect with and embrace.

Finding purpose does not have to be complicated. One does not need to go to an ashram, find a guru, or meditate for days to find purpose in their work. However, what one does need to do is understand their set of activities, the people they work with, and the outcomes and goals of their work. If one of those elements resonates with them, the employee can find purpose in their work.

The work has to be impactful for the organization, wherein the organization's outcomes are aligned with that work.

Finally, the person doing the work should have adequate skills to be effective in that line of work. When the purpose and adequate skills the individual possesses intersect with the needs and goals of the organization or the team they are on, this lands them squarely in the blue zone of their workplace.

The best outcomes for the organization and the employees happen in that blue zone. It would be naive to assume that all work by all employees will be in the blue zone. However, as organizations move to a more skills-based approach to mapping work for employees, the relative size of the blue zone expands in the organization, leading to a more engaged workforce and better outcomes for the organization at a lower cost, both in terms of resources and money.

Every organizational leader and every individual in the organization must aspire to be part of the blue zone. The blue zone of work is where everything aligns.

For the organization, the blue zone also represents the opportunities where the impact is meaningful to the organizational goals and objectives. The activities in this zone are generally directly related to the work that is aligned with the strategy of the organization that their leaders and managers have identified.

It's that Goldilocks zone, where everyone thrives: The organization is getting the best work from their people for the things that matter to the organization's success. People like and enjoy what they are working on, and they are good at this area of work. In fact, they are getting better every day since they are passionate about this area, and it drives them. This is an area where they may be in the "flow" state a lot because they are so deeply involved. Working in the blue zone reduces the impact of long hours because the work is so deep and meaningful to the individual that they don't necessarily feel the burnout or fatigue felt while working long hours in the red zone or the purple zone.

CULTIVATING PURPOSE

As the individual evolves in their life and work, their desires and purpose may change as well. In fact, Frankl argues that meaning is not a static or fixed entity but is unique to each individual. He highlighted the importance of taking responsibility for one's own life and embracing the challenges and opportunities that come with it: "What man actually needs is not a tensionless state but rather the striving and struggling for some goal worthy of him. What he needs is not the discharge of tension at any cost but the call of a potential meaning waiting to be fulfilled by him."[5]

While much of Frankl's research and approach are based on patients at his psychiatric wards and his own experience of pain, loss, and suffering at the Nazi concentration camps, his belief system is still valid at the workplace.

It is important to find a zone of purpose and meaning for an individual even when they are at work. Significant research has been done that now provides direct evidence on psychological well-being, physical well-being, and overall life satisfaction on doing purposeful work, even if it is something one does to pay their bills. One of the ways in which an individual finds meaning in life is through work that is creative in nature, adequately challenging, and aligned to a purpose and goal greater than themselves.

The good news is that people at your workplace are looking for that blue zone. In fact, a LinkedIn survey shows that 71 percent of people are looking for work where they can align their values to the organization's values and purpose.[6] Frank Martela and Anne B. Pessi argue in their important research, "Significant Work Is about Self-Realization and Broader Purpose: Defining the Key Dimensions of Meaningful Work," in *Frontiers in Psychology*, that in the modern era, people find meaning at the workplace more than ever before.[7] They are not simply looking for a paycheck.

EVALUATING PURPOSE

Determining whether an employee is finding meaning and purpose in their work can be a subjective assessment, but there are several indicators that can help managers gauge their engagement and satisfaction and whether they are finding meaning in their work.

The first sign of purpose is the employee's level of satisfaction. A genuinely engaged employee will exhibit higher levels of satisfaction in their role. If not in words, their level of satisfaction will be apparent in their body language. Most often, they will express enthusiasm for the work and raise their hand for new activities and challenges. They will also ask a lot of questions that will help them get clarity in their work and participate actively in team discussions.

Whether their goals align with the team's or organization's purpose will also indicate the employee's own connection with purpose. As a manager, you should know whether your employee's personal goals align with the organization's and your team's mission and values, and you must communicate that connection to your team members. When they see their work contributing to a larger purpose or cause, the employee is more likely to find their work meaningful.

Personal growth and development are also crucial parts of an employee realizing their purpose. Employees who find meaning in their work will actively seek additional opportunities for growth and development. They will seek out challenging projects on their own volition so that they can learn and develop new skills.

To go a step further, an employee who recognizes their purpose will generally be proactive. Motivated employees tend to take initiative and offer new ideas to improve processes or solve problems. They will demonstrate a sense of ownership and dedication to their work, actively seeking ways to make an impact.

Finally, a purposeful employee will exhibit a positive attitude. They will display positive relationships with their teammates. If an employee enjoys strong connections, collaboration, and a supportive work environment, it can enhance their overall satisfaction and sense of purpose.

Remember that individual perceptions of meaningful work can vary, and what motivates one person may not resonate with another. Regular communication, one-on-one discussions, and employee feedback surveys can provide valuable insights into their experience and help gauge their level of engagement and purpose in their role.

However, if you don't notice these behaviors, the employee is lacking meaning in their work. Without meaningful work, the employee is still actively working in the purple zone or, miserably, in the red zone. This is neither good for the individual nor for the organization.

IN THE ZONE?

Knowing whether an employee is in the red zone or purple zone is one thing that separates good managers from average ones. A good manager will be attentive and observant to gauge whether an employee is unhappy with their work or lacking the necessary skills for their role. There are many indicators that can help the manager identify red zone issues.

Be on the lookout for decreased productivity. If you notice a significant drop in an employee's productivity or a consistent decline in their work outcomes, it could be a sign of disengagement, usually due to their inability to find meaning in that work or significant gaps in their skill to perform it.

Missing deadlines and a lack of quality are also key signs that your employee is in the wrong zone. Frequent missed deadlines or a decline in the quality of work delivered by an employee may indicate that they are not adequately skilled or motivated in their role or the set of activities they are working on. This could be due to a lack of understanding, inadequate training, or disengagement.

If an employee displays a lack of enthusiasm, motivation, or drive in their work, it might indicate that they are not finding meaning in that work or there is a mismatch between their skills and the tasks assigned to them. They may appear disinterested or disengaged during meetings or contribute less to team discussions.

When an employee becomes unhappy or lacks the necessary skills, they may exhibit increased absenteeism or tardiness. This behavior could be the result of demotivation, dissatisfaction, or an attempt to avoid challenging tasks.

If an employee starts to withdraw from teamwork, avoids collaborative projects, or shies away from committing to working with others in the team, it may be a sign of dissatisfaction or feeling inadequate in their role. They may not feel comfortable seeking help or contributing to team efforts, or they don't find meaning in their work.

REZONING TO BLUE

The manager's role then becomes identifying and working with the employee to find the blue zone of work. This is not always easy, but it is important to address. Many bad managers will choose to ignore the problem or wish it away. They will assume this is a temporary issue and not bring it up with the employee in their discussions for lack of skill in having hard conversations. But these problems seldom go away on their own. Most of these issues can easily be worked out by adjusting the type of work the employee does or providing more clarity on how their work matters to the larger team and the organization.

Some of these issues may have occurred in the hiring process, where you hired an employee who was desperate for a paycheck and not necessarily motivated to work in your organization. In those cases, unless there is meaningful work in your team or the organization that can motivate and inspire the employee to be effective and engaged, you may have to transition them out of the organization.

In most such situations, however, the employee is in the purple zone, where either their work does not provide meaning or purpose for them or their skills are inadequate.

In the case where they cannot find meaning or purpose, the manager has to provide clarity on the big picture and the overall goals and mission of the organization. Simon Sinek, in his best-selling book *Start with the Why*, talks about this: "Great companies don't hire skilled people and motivate them; they hire already motivated people and inspire them. People are either motivated or they are not. Unless you give motivated people something to believe in, something bigger than their job to work toward, they will motivate themselves to find a new job, and you'll be stuck with whoever's left."[8]

However, a blue zone does not come to fruition only because the individual is finding meaningful work and purpose in their activities at work; the organization also needs to benefit directly from that individual's work. In fact, the odds of an individual finding meaningful work increase when the organization's goal and purpose are also aligned to that work.

To do that effectively, organizations need to be transparent about their business strategy and their overall purpose. Many organizations are not very transparent about their goals. In most organizations, the frontline employees have very little understanding or appreciation of what the organization's goals are.

In an important study done by Erik Berggren and Rob Bernshteyn, the authors argued that organizational transparency drives company performance.[9] Their study posited that, in the current era of rapid change, people at these organizations need to be strategically aligned to the organization's strategy, which is changing more frequently than ever before. This alignment is only effective if the organizations are transparent about their strategy. The researchers maintain that this allows employees at these organizations to undertake the relevant change actions to stay aligned to the organizational strategy.

To promote transparency about goals and work objectives, organizations and their leaders should follow some of these best practices:

- Start by clearly communicating the mission and vision. Ensure that the organization's mission and vision statements are well defined and accessible to all employees. These statements should outline the purpose, values, and long-term goals of the organization.

- Next, set clear goals for teams and individuals. Clearly communicate these goals to all employees, explaining how they align with the organization's overall objectives.

- Provide regular updates on the progress of organizational goals and, in the cases of a team, your team goals, and be transparent in your communications. Don't be afraid to share both successes and challenges to foster a culture of transparency and accountability.

- Lead by example. That transparency goes all the way up: Managers and leaders should lead by example by being transparent about their own goals and decision-making processes. When leaders demonstrate transparency, it encourages their employees to do the same.

- Create an environment where open and honest communication is encouraged. Establish channels such as town hall meetings, suggestion boxes, feedback surveys, or digital collaboration platforms to allow employees to share their ideas, concerns, and suggestions regarding organizational goals and work objectives.

- Foster a culture of collaboration and knowledge sharing across departments and teams. Encourage employees to work together on projects, participate in cross-functional initiatives, and share insights and best practices. This promotes transparency and a collective understanding of organizational goals. Actively avoid talent hoarding when the talent can be better aligned with a different team.

You will have noticed a pattern here: Transparent communication is crucial to ensuring that your team is engaged. If they don't trust you or can't see your purpose, they won't be able to see their own either.

In the case where skills are lacking because the work evolved over time, managers must focus on development for the employee. Skill development is an essential part of the organization's people practices, and every manager should own it for their team. With the rapid changes in technology and work practices, skills requirements will change over time, so it is not unusual to expect people will need training and development in new skills to be effective in their roles.

To find the blue zone, the managers and their employees need to work together to understand what drives the organization and what drives the employees. There is a workbook at the end of this book that talks about an assessment the employee and the manager can take to align themselves with the blue zone of work. This assessment takes stock of what the employee is passionate about and the areas where the employee is skilled. The manager uses the assessment to identify key areas the organization needs people to work on.

As we discussed earlier, finding the blue zone is not an easy task, as both the manager and the individual may not necessarily agree on what they believe is the area of strength and passion for an employee. There may be a strong belief that an employee has a stronger skill set than the manager believes to be true. This can cause friction and anxiety between the manager and the employee in working on aligning with true blue zone areas.

A mutual environment of trust needs to be established between the manager and the employee to build a common framework and understanding of what the blue zone areas are.

KEY TAKEAWAYS

- Having a sense of purpose in one's job can lead to greater engagement, motivation, and fulfillment in the workplace.

- To be in the blue zone at work, individuals should align their personal sense of purpose and skills with the goals and objectives of the organization. When these elements align, it results in meaningful work that benefits both the employee and the organization.

- Organizations should promote transparency by clearly communicating their mission, vision, and goals. Additionally, they should invest in skill development to ensure employees have the necessary skills to excel in their roles. Transparent communication and skill development contribute to creating a culture where employees can find their blue zone.

7

HIRING FOR THE BLUE ZONE

You don't hire for skills; you hire for attitude. You can always teach skills.

—Simon Sinek

When building a team, the biggest mistakes are made in the hiring process. Whether that new hire is found external to the organization or from an internal team, managers in a rush to fill the role make a hire because they look good on paper or are great interviewees. In my own experience of hiring several dozen individuals, I can look back and see where I made most of my mistakes. I can categorize the reasons as:

- Rush to fill the role because of a client requirement

- Getting impressed by the packaging and presentation

- Not following a thorough process

In each of these cases where I failed to hire the right individual for the role, it was because I was not actively assessing the candidate for the blue zone. I have spent most of my career in fast-paced environments, first at Ernst & Young, and then in two different technology start-ups. In today's fast-paced world, it's all too common for individuals and organizations to rush into filling a role simply because of a client requirement or competitive environment. I found myself getting impressed by the packaging and presentation, often neglecting the importance of a thorough process. It's as if I became so infatuated with the superficial aspects that I overlooked the essence of what truly matters in that role for the individual to be successful.

Impressions can be deceiving. I was easily swayed by flashy resumes, polished portfolios, top colleges, big brand experience, and charismatic interviews, all of which create a captivating impression. But what lies beneath the surface? Are we truly taking the time to delve deep into a candidate's qualifications and skills, and more importantly, their potential to adapt as the role changes? Are we assessing the cultural fit within the organization? Unfortunately, when I rushed to fill a role, I often neglected these crucial aspects.

In one particular example, I was swayed by a flashy resume and background. It still haunts me. The particular individual had the best pedigree: They came from a top-ten university in engineering and a top-five university for business. The individual also came recommended from a trusted source and had worked at a big software company. On paper, we felt that we hit the jackpot on a candidate who would propel our organization forward.

During the interview process, the candidate gave vague answers to our questions on key accomplishments in their last few roles and redirected when we asked about their approach to strategy execution—but we brushed it off. This was a key error in our approach to the interview process. We hired the individual in this important executive role at a nosebleed compensation anyway.

In a few weeks, it was clear that the new leader's team was in disarray, there was no movement on important projects, and there was a lack of clarity on vision and purpose. Even then, we assumed it was something wrong with our approach or the team. We spent an enormous amount of management bandwidth trying to figure out how to make the team work well.

Within a few months, it was clear that the person was a bad hire. What may have worked in a big organization didn't work for our agile start-up environment. Such mistakes are costly, especially for a start-up, which has limited resources, is pressed for time, and is in a highly competitive market.

There are severe consequences to making a mistake in hiring. According to a study by SHRM, the cost of a bad hire can range from 50 percent to several times the employee's annual salary.[1] The US Department of Labor estimates that the average cost of a bad hire is around 30 percent of the individual's first-year earnings.[2] But the costs aren't only monetary: A CareerBuilder survey found that 74 percent of companies reported making a bad hire, with 37 percent stating that it resulted in a loss in productivity and 22 percent indicating a negative impact on client relationships.[3]

By skipping critical steps, such as reference verifications, assessments, and comprehensive interviews, we expose ourselves to potential risks, both to the organization as well as the individual's career. Our organization's services and products end up being subpar, and we may incur significant costs for the organization as a result. On the other hand, the individual may have been a better fit somewhere else where they would flourish in that role and build a great career. We may inad-vertently hire individuals who lack the necessary skills, competence, or ethical standards required for the role. This hasty decision-making can lead to costly mistakes, compromised teamwork, and even damage to our reputation.

Matt Poepsel has this to say on the topic: "Personality assessments help a great deal with this. It's also important to properly train interview team members as they don't hire often, and too many don't hire well."[4]

So how do we overcome these challenges? It begins with recognizing that the superficial is fleeting, while substance endures. Our pedigree engineering leader may have been a great hire for a different organiza-tion, but it clearly was not for our start-up at that time. Performance in a blue zone is not just about what is on a resume but what fits well within your culture, your work dynamics, and the outcomes you and the employee want in their role.

We must resist the allure of immediate gratification and invest the time and effort needed to thoroughly assess candidates. By implementing a robust hiring process that includes in-depth interviews, comprehensive assessments, and meticulous reference checks, we can make informed decisions and secure the best talent for our organizations.

THE JOB DESCRIPTION

In many cases, bad hiring starts at the job description itself. The job description of a given role is often incorrect in accurately describing the role. Lou Adler, CEO and founder of consulting firm Hiring Learning Systems, argues that job descriptions are preventing organizations from hiring the best candidate for a role.[5]

According to Adler, there are several problems with traditional job descriptions. Traditional job descriptions have the following issues:

Vague or Generic Language

Job descriptions often use generic language that fails to provide a clear understanding of the actual role and its requirements. This can result in attracting a wide range of candidates, including those who may not possess the specific skills or qualifications needed for success in the position.[6]

A common error we see in job descriptions is generic phrases like *excellent communication skills, a great team player,* or *manages work effectively.* These types of statements, which most hiring managers—including myself—have been guilty of, provide no mechanism of appealing to the right candidate or qualifying one. The generic nature of the "qualifications" means that every candidate is qualified and that you haven't articulated what the job will actually require.

Excess Focus on Skills and Experience over Potential

Traditional job descriptions tend to focus heavily on a candidate's past experience and skills rather than their potential and ability to learn and grow. This approach can limit the talent pool and overlook candidates who may have transferable skills or a strong aptitude for the role.[7]

I often see an alphabet soup of skills and experience added to a job description, such as *ten years of team management* or *bachelor's required.* The number of years or having a bachelor's degree tells you very little about how good they have been in their role. In many cases, the recruiting manager is weeding out perfectly capable candidates from the interview process.

Lack of Performance Expectations

Many job descriptions fail to clearly outline the performance expectations and desired outcomes for the role. Instead of specifying what success looks like, they often list a series of tasks and responsibilities without providing a holistic view of how the position contributes to the organization's goals.[8]

Many job descriptions I see lack performance outcomes and have generic statements on expectations, such as *must be able to create and maintain a strong culture.* Many job descriptions I have seen completely miss having expectations in the first place, instead only describing the duties of the role.

Absence of Impact and Purpose

Job descriptions often lack emphasis on the broader impact of the role and how it aligns with the organization's purpose and mission. This can result in a lack of motivation and engagement among candidates who are seeking meaningful work that makes a difference.[9]

Like the preceding examples, most job descriptions seem to be generated by ChatGPT, are generic, and do not differentiate from others competing for great candidates.

Lengthy and Uninspiring

Traditional job descriptions are often lengthy, filled with jargon, and lacking in excitement. They fail to capture the attention and imagination of potential candidates, making it difficult to stand out in a competitive job market.[10]

Some of these job descriptions add everything the person does in the role—including activities that are just routine, like showing up to work on time. The problem with such job descriptions is that including this kind of information drowns out the key differentiators or outcomes the candidate will really need to achieve in the role. The best job descriptions should be no more than necessary: Cut out the fluff and flowery language. The focus should on the key requirements, achievements, and the results the candidate will be responsible for.

To address these problems, Adler suggests focusing on performance profiles instead of traditional job descriptions.[11] Performance profiles clearly define the key objectives, expected outcomes, and critical skills required for success in a role. They provide a clearer picture of what the person needs to accomplish, allowing for a more accurate assessment of candidates' fit and potential. This approach shifts the focus from past experiences to future performance and fosters a more inclusive and effective recruitment process.

Conventional job descriptions, centered on skills, primarily outline the requisite qualifications and general skills for a given position. For instance, when seeking a sales employee, a typical job description might include this type of language:

- Mandatory college degree
- Strong ability to communicate
- Three to five years of sales experience required
- Willingness to acquire in-depth product knowledge
- Attention to detail

While these criteria are valuable, they are overly broad and focused on the desired qualities in a candidate rather than specific accomplishments or performance metrics.

In contrast, a performance-based profile shifts the emphasis to the outcomes that must be attained and provides a more nuanced understanding of the responsibilities and daily tasks crucial for success in the role. Instead of generic candidate qualities, a performance profile will include more precise measures of success, such as these:

- Attain a monthly target of closing fifteen new customers.

- Effectively prioritize and manage multiple projects.

- Systematically organize and transmit sales forms and payment transactions to the accounting department within two to three business days.

- Meet a quarterly sales quota of $200,000.

The distinction between these two approaches is evident, and each type of job description is likely to attract candidates with varying skill sets and qualities. Employing performance profile examples in job descriptions can significantly impact the quality and diversity of applications received.

ASSESSING EXCITEMENT, DESIRE, AND ASPIRATIONS

Another aspect to consider is whether the candidate is applying for a role merely because they are a good fit for the role requirements rather than being enthusiastic about the role and having a desire to learn and grow, an important factor for several reasons.

First, candidates who are genuinely passionate about a role and have a desire to learn and grow are more likely to be motivated and engaged in their work. They are driven by intrinsic factors, such as personal development and the desire to contribute meaningfully, which can lead to higher job satisfaction and productivity.

When candidates are genuinely enthusiastic about a role, they are also more likely to commit to it for the long term. They are willing to invest time and effort into developing their skills and expertise, which can result in higher employee retention rates and reduced turnover costs for the organization.

Candidates with a genuine desire to learn and grow are also more likely to be adaptable and open to new challenges and opportunities. They are willing to step out of their comfort zones, acquire new skills, and embrace change. This mindset is particularly valuable in today's rapidly evolving and dynamic work environments.

Finally, truly enthusiastic candidates create value. Because they are eager to learn and grow, they bring a positive energy and a fresh perspective to their work and they are more likely to seek innovative solutions, embrace continuous improvement, and contribute to the organization's overall success. Their enthusiasm can inspire and motivate their colleagues as well.

Gordon Rapkin says this about getting the best candidate: "It is almost impossible to know with certainty who the best candidate is, but I focus on personality and look for the best athlete. I believe we can teach most job skills, but we can't teach personality or core beliefs."[12]

While skills, experience, and even potential can be assessed in a good interview process or can be taught later, how do you assess personality traits like desire and aspiration to excel in that role?

To assess these personality traits, we must venture beyond conventional interview techniques to truly uncover a job candidate's inner drive. We must delve deep into their experiences. We must pose open-ended questions that kindle their storytelling instincts, inviting them to share specific instances when their fervor ignited and propelled them to excel. Let us inquire: "Tell us of a time when your heart swelled with excitement for a project or task. How did you manifest this enthusiasm, and what were the outcomes?"

There are different ways a candidate may respond to this question. In one case, where the person is not very passionate about the role, they might give a vague answer such as this:

I was called to do a repair project at a client's factory that made soda cans. It was a tough job since it took several hours, but I was able to diagnose the problem quickly, and I was excited to be able to fix it in less than a week. My district manager praised my work, and I got an extra bonus that year.

Or the candidate could answer more like this:

I was called to diagnose a problem at a client's soda can factory. The problem had stopped one of their key production lines. As a kid, I had always been passionate about machinery and fixing things. This was right up my alley. It took several hours, but I figured out that one of the processors in the computer board had overheated and burned out. I called the manufacturer and got a replacement shipped overnight, so the next morning at 7 a.m. I got back in to replace the part. By 8:30, the line was operational. To see the smiles on the faces of the foreman and the plant manager gave me joy. It is one of many such incidents, but this kind of work really is what I strive to do every day.

The response and the passion behind the response can help you determine if the person is the type of candidate you want to hire.

Moreover, let us explore their personal career aspirations. By inquiring about their long-term objectives and how this role aligns with their dreams, we unravel the tapestry of their innermost desires. For those who possess a genuine yearning to grow and excel, their responses will paint a vivid picture of their ambitions and reveal the profound connection between their trajectory and the role at hand.

We must not overlook the significance of curiosity and proactivity in our evaluation. By unraveling the candidate's intellectual appetite and zest for knowledge, we gain insight into their inner drive. How do they stay attuned to the pulse of their industry? How have they embraced learning opportunities in the past? These inquiries will unravel their voracious appetite for growth and their unwavering commitment to staying ahead.

For example, to a question like "How will you improve our marketing?" a subpar candidate will respond with generic answers one can find on the internet. They might say, "I'd implement demand gen campaigns and influencer marketing or spend money on paid campaigns." A thoughtful candidate would ask more questions, diagnosing the problem instead of offering solutions without fully understanding the problem.

Yet, words alone may not suffice. Nonverbal cues hold a profound language of their own. As astute observers, pay attention to the candidate's body language, tone of voice, and overall enthusiasm during the interview. Through these subtle expressions, we can glimpse the fire within, the unspoken passion that fuels their desire to excel. Often, that depends on the role. For example, if the position you are interviewing for is in client management, but the candidate comes across fidgety, does not maintain eye contact, or seems bored, then they may not be a good fit for the role. However, that may not be a big issue for an engineering role.

And in our quest for the best fit, reference checks will unravel insights as well. By reaching out to the candidate's previous supervisors or colleagues, we can uncover rich insights into their zeal, their hunger to learn, and their commitment to their craft. Usually, when a reference is provided by the candidate, it will be a favorable one, so the questions to ask a reference would be for examples of behavior exhibited that are relevant to the role. Instead of asking generic questions like "How did the candidate perform in their role at *xyz*?" ask questions like "Is there an example of a situation where the candidate went above and beyond?" and listen to how specific that response is. Another effective question would be whether the reference would hire this person again. Ask them to rate the candidate on a scale of 1–10. Because of the candidate's likely positive relationship with the reference, anything less than an 8 would be a red flag in this case, for me.

It is important to realize that reference checks are simply one of many tools to understand whether the candidate is a good fit for the role. A questionable review may indicate that the person was not a good fit for a role at a prior organization, but that shouldn't automatically disqualify the candidate. The reverse is also a true: A good fit at their previous organization doesn't mean they'll be a good fit for yours. Also, reference checks allow you to see whether the candidate's description of their strengths and experiences aligns with those provided in the reference check.

Remember that assessing excitement, desire, and aspirations necessitates an artful blend of probing questions, perceptive observation, and diligent reference checks. While there are no guarantees, this gives one a better chance of hiring someone in the blue zone.

HIRING FROM WITHIN

When we contemplate the task of filling a role within our organization, let us not overlook the hidden treasure that lies in internal hires. There are instances when individuals are promoted or moved laterally within the organization, and this path holds immense potential. But in our zeal to hire internal talent, we may also make the mistake of moving people to roles because they want to get promoted or the role appears to be more glamorous.

Let us not be blind to a peculiar but painfully real phenomenon known as *the Peter principle*. With a touch of humor, but rooted in undeniable truth, this principle reveals that individuals within a hierarchical structure often ascend to a level of "respective incompetence." It is a cautionary tale, warning us that promotions are frequently bestowed upon individuals based on their past successes, yet their competence may fall short when faced with new challenges. The skills that brought success in one role do not necessarily guarantee proficiency in another.

A common real-world example of the Peter principle is that of leadership often promoting people to managerial positions because that person was excellent as an individual contributor. The skills required to be a manager are different from those required to be a successful individual contributor in a given role. The challenge of leading people as a team will require skill development in that area, which may not have been necessary in their prior role. A well-designed development program that includes training and active coaching can help set them up to lead a team.

It is crucial for organizations to acknowledge this inherent danger. Titles such as Director or VP can possess an allure that tempts individuals seeking career growth or a badge of honor and bragging rights to their friends and family. However, we must exercise caution and discernment. The siren song of prestigious titles may seduce us into promoting individuals who may not possess the necessary aptitude for their new-found responsibilities.

Let us recognize that wrong promotions occur more frequently than we may realize within our organizational realms. We must be vigilant in our quest to discern true competence and potential. The path to excellence lies not in the temptation of flashy titles but in the earnest evaluation of an individual's abilities, character, and adaptability. It is inevitable that, despite our best intentions and efforts, we end up promoting the wrong person to a role. If it is determined that coaching and training may not be sufficient and that it is indeed a wrong person in the role, it is better to swallow our pride and accept that we made a mistake. We can then have an honest conversation with that individual before more damage is done to the morale of the team. In many cases, there may be other roles within the organization that the person may be a fit for, or there may be other roles outside the organization. In some rare cases, the person may not take this personally and would move back to their original role. Making these changes so that the individual is performing in the blue zone requires a thoughtful and empathetic approach.

HIRING FOR THE FUTURE

The last thing is to consider that you are not only hiring for today's role but also for the individual to adapt and fit in as the role evolves over time. In our quest to build exceptional teams, let us not confine our focus solely to the present requirements of a role. We must extend our gaze toward the future, envisioning the evolution and growth that lies ahead for the organization and your teams. Remember that we are not merely seeking someone to fulfill today's needs, but looking for an individual who possesses the capacity to adapt and seamlessly integrate as the role unfolds and transforms over time.

In the ever-changing landscape of business, organizations are not stagnant entities. They are dynamic organisms, continually evolving to navigate the challenges and seize the opportunities that arise. Roles that exist today may undergo metamorphosis tomorrow, as the demands of the marketplace, technological advancements, and customer needs demand a constant state of adaptation.

Therefore, it is vital to approach the hiring process with a forward-thinking perspective. We must seek individuals who possess not only the skills and desire to excel in the present role but also the innate ability to embrace change, learn new skills, and thrive amid uncertainty.

Just as a chameleon adjusts its colors to harmonize with its surroundings, we must seek candidates who possess a natural inclination toward versatility and flexibility. Such individuals are not bound by the limitations of the current role but possess the visionary mindset to anticipate future needs and actively contribute to the transformation that lies ahead. The best way to assess that ability is to delve into their prior experiences in transitioning when situations changed and when adaptation and growth were required. Look for evidence of the individual realizing that conditions had changed and that they had to learn, grow their skills, and adapt their processes. For an internal hire, it is easier to observe that, but in the case of external hires, it will be imperative to ask questions about when the person may have displayed that ability and to validate that evidence with their growth history in their career and with their references.

This deliberate pursuit will uncover the true gems, the individuals who will not merely fit into the role, but who will shape and redefine it, contributing to a culture of continuous growth and unwavering excellence. Your odds of finding the candidate who will not only fit the blue zone today but also in the future increase dramatically.

KEY TAKEAWAYS

- The biggest mistakes organizations make when building a team often occur during the hiring process. Rushing to fill a role, being impressed by surface-level qualities, and not following a thorough hiring process are common pitfalls.

- To make informed hiring decisions, it's crucial to assess a candidate's genuine excitement for the role and their aspirations to learn and grow. This involves asking probing questions, observing nonverbal cues, and conducting diligent reference checks.

- When hiring, organizations should consider not only the immediate needs of a role but also the candidate's potential to adapt and thrive as the role evolves over time. Seek individuals with the capacity to embrace change and contribute to the organization's long-term growth and success.

8

DEVELOPING PEOPLE
FOR THE BLUE ZONE

*Success is no accident. It is hard work, perseverance, learning, studying,
sacrifice, and most of all, love of what you are doing or learning to do.*

—Pele

I f *success* in your talent strategy is marked by getting people to work in
the blue zone, the only way to achieve this will be through deliberate
efforts. The second law of thermodynamics states that, without intervention, entropy—disorder, decay, and uncertainty—will increase over
time. This also applies to talent in your teams. Over time, people who
you may have thought were in the blue end of the ikigai Venn diagram
end up in the purple zone, and if they are not actively engaged, in the
red zone.

When I was in graduate school, majoring in international business
and finance, one of the ideal career paths that I envisioned was being a

financial analyst and rising up to be a CFO. I had been trading the stock market and avidly following company performances, their strategy, etc., since high school. The world of financial modeling, financial engineering, and competitive strategies fascinated me.

So, naturally, during my internship program, which lasted a summer and a full semester (about seven months), I chose a position in a finance department at a major automotive manufacturer. It was a great learning experience. I was diving deep into complex Excel spreadsheets, calculating and forecasting and building macros (a type of programming language for Excel). One change in inventory forecasting or pricing could flow through the chain of interconnected sheets. It was such an exciting experience that I spent the whole Thanksgiving weekend (including Thanksgiving Day) working at the plant offices. I was in the blue zone. I thoroughly enjoyed what I was doing. The organization got an effective employee in the form of a dedicated intern who worked through weekends to help build better budgets and financial forecasts.

But by Christmas, I was spent. I could not go to sleep without Excel spreadsheets flying in my head. After my internship ended around that time, it was clear that I would be miserable in the long run with a job in corporate finance, working with numbers day in and day out. I was good at it, and naturally skilled due to my math and engineering background. But I did not get to do enough of the creative thinking and approaches that I enjoyed so much. I also did not get to interact with a lot of people, and staring at the computer twelve hours a day was taking a toll on my mind. I could not sleep without dreaming of spreadsheets and waking up to solve the financial model that I could not fix the night before.

I had slipped out of the blue zone and into the purple zone. I decided not to pursue a career in corporate finance, even though I likely could have been quite successful at it. It is not uncommon for people to slip out of the blue zone. However, it is quite possible that I could have stayed in the blue zone in corporate finance if I had mixed up my financial modeling with some other creative endeavors within the realm of finance or some other interdisciplinary field, like marketing or engineering and finance.

Over time, I realized that my blue zone of work is actually quite varied, involving work on strategy, process development, and data analysis, as well as work with people. In essence, my blue zone is not found specializing in one specific subject but as a generalist with some level of specializing in process, data, and analysis.

In my current line of work running Engagedly, an HR technology company, I actively deal with finance for our own needs in budgeting, forecasting, and executing our financial plan for growth and long-term success, but it's not the only thing I do. I also work on our marketing strategy and our product strategy, talking to a lot of our customers and sales prospects, thereby indulging in different interdisciplinary activities that keep me in the blue zone, where I find meaning and purpose in my work, and Engagedly benefits as well.

People and interests change over time, as is evidenced by my own change in career over time from being an engineer, software programmer, and financial analyst, to a management and process consultant, to being a technology entrepreneur.

There is no one fixed blue zone for any individual, and the zones can shift over time depending on the work, the organization's culture and management, as well as the individual's changing needs and desires over time. Various environmental and societal factors can have a major impact on an individual, as evidenced by the workplace changes that have occurred since the pandemic. This can unexpectedly shift the zone of work people were in.

WHY ARE PEOPLE QUITTING?

Toward the end of the pandemic, we saw a large exodus of people from their jobs. Many of them had realized they were not in a blue zone. Over time, as people slip out of their blue zones, they will eventually quit. The blue zone may not just include the actual work but also the environmental factors. People quit their jobs where they didn't get fulfillment or didn't feel respected. There are usually several factors that drive people to quit their job. Let's look at a few.

Lack of Fulfillment

Many individuals seek meaning and purpose in their work. When they find that their current job doesn't align with their values, passions, or long-term goals, they may feel unfulfilled. This lack of fulfillment can lead to dissatisfaction, leading to disengagement and a desire to explore other opportunities that offer more meaningful work.

Matt Poepsel believes that "when employees disengage from their work, they're sending us a message. They can't see opportunities for growth, they lack supportive relationships with coworkers, or they can't find the inherent meaning in what they're doing—sometimes all three!"[1]

Limited Growth and Development

People often desire opportunities for growth and advancement in their careers. If they feel their current job doesn't provide adequate chances for learning, acquiring new skills, or progressing professionally, they may seek alternatives elsewhere.

Lack of Respect and Appreciation

Feeling valued and respected in the workplace is crucial for job satisfaction. If an individual consistently experiences disrespect, mistreatment, or lack of appreciation from colleagues or superiors, it can erode their motivation and overall happiness at work. Such negative experiences may prompt them to quit in search of a more supportive and respectful environment.

Toxic Work Culture

A toxic work culture characterized by excessive stress, micromanagement, poor communication, or lack of work-life balance can significantly impact an employee's well-being. When the work environment becomes excessively negative or unhealthy, individuals often decide to leave in order to protect their mental and physical health.

In fact, several research studies support this assertion. In a comprehensive review article for the *Annual Review of Psychology*, authors Timothy Judge and John Kammeyer-Mueller examined various factors that contribute to job attitudes, including job satisfaction and fulfillment.[2] They concluded that job satisfaction is one of the critical determinants of an employee's loyalty and their advocacy for the organization

In an article for the *Journal of Management*, authors Russell Cropanzano and Marie Mitchell explored social exchange theory, which includes the notion of reciprocity and fairness in workplace relationships, including respect and appreciation.[3] Social exchange theory posits that social interactions are based on the principle of reciprocity. Individuals engage in exchanges with others—in this case, the organization—with the expectation of receiving benefits or rewards in return for their actions. The theory suggests that people are motivated to maintain relationships that offer a fair and equitable balance of rewards and costs. In a culture where people feel fairness and respect for their work, we should expect better motivation from the employees in their work.

In their influential paper, "The 'What' and 'Why' of Goal Pursuits: Human Needs and the Self-Determination of Behavior," authors Edward Deci and Richard Ryan discussed the concept of self-determination theory, which emphasizes the importance of intrinsic motivation and the fulfillment of psychological needs, such as autonomy, competence, and relatedness, in the workplace.[4] Deci and Ryan argue that when these psychological needs are satisfied, individuals are more likely to experience high-quality motivation and well-being. In contrast, when these needs are thwarted, the individuals may experience lower motivation, reduced well-being, and various negative outcomes.

In an article for the *Journal of Vocational Behavior*, authors Hakanen, Perhoniemi, and Toppinen-Tanner examine the relationship between job resources, work engagement, and personal initiative, highlighting the positive effects of fulfilling work experiences.[5] The researchers concluded that the better job resources employees had, the better work engagement was demonstrated by the employee, and it led to a higher personal initiative.

A work culture should support fairness, higher levels of autonomy in a role—that is, less micromanagement—and access to adequate resources, including management support. When there is a better perception of management support for people in their role in these aspects, the work culture promotes higher levels of motivation, employee advocacy, and—ultimately—better outcomes for both the organization and the employee.

THE ROLE OF MANAGEMENT

One of the key roles of a manager is to develop and grow their team members and get a pulse on what is driving their job satisfaction and fulfillment at work. Conversely, it is also important that the manager identify early signs of disengagement by identifying an employee's workplace behaviors.

Early in my career at Ernst & Young, as a management consultant, I was working on a high-stakes project for a major financial institution whose brick-and-mortar business was under threat from online banking and self-trading platforms. They had to quickly reinvent themselves to allow their customers self-service and the ability to trade stocks and options online or risk losing the tech-savvy generation to online trading platforms and banks.

This was an exciting time for us in the financial services industry, especially for me since this was exactly the kind of challenge a twenty-something like me would seek. However, a few months into the project, we were slipping behind schedule. The systems we were developing turned out to be way more complicated than we originally thought because of high dependence on legacy mainframe–type systems, which were not easy to fix.

Our team and our banking client teams were starting to get a bit demoralized. What started off as great blue zones for many individuals were quickly becoming purple zones for many of us. There was a lot of finger-pointing and interoffice politicking, as well as gossip, which never bodes well for a good office culture.

We got a new manager, Mark, to help turn the ship around. One of his biggest tasks was to build back up the morale of the team and bring all our issues to the forefront. His job was to bring us back into our blue zones.

One of the most impactful practices he did was a daily check-in at 9:00 a.m. where all the leads—I was leading the business analysis team at that time—did a stand-up. Each day, we went through a three-question check:

- What worked for us yesterday?
- What will we be working on to get this project back on track?
- What challenges prevent us from doing that?

As simple as this sounds, going through this exercise with a handful of us made us feel that our work mattered and that there was a bigger purpose behind our individual work. This also brought all the inter-team issues to the forefront, so the back-alley gossiping was minimized, creating a better overall culture.

Post-Pandemic Concerns

Before the pandemic, a manager could easily walk around and meet their team members around the watercooler or at the coffee machine. In a post-pandemic era, where the world has gone flat and virtual, a manager and their team may be distributed across time zones and different countries. This poses a unique challenge for a manager to be effective. My manager Mark's technique is something that, while highly effective, is hard to do when your team is across different countries and time zones. These talks might appear to be about work, but they were actually helping us become better leaders for our teams. We were developing in our career as better managers.

In today's workplace, where hybrid work is the norm, these types of stand-ups are one of the best ways managers can adapt. They can do this through daily or weekly team pulse check-ins and one-on-ones using video-conferencing software. These interactions create opportunities to discuss progress, address challenges, and provide guidance in a more personalized manner. It's like staying connected and offering support while using technology to enhance the process.

Mapping Career Development

Yet another strategy that has proven effective is engaging in a dedicated one-on-one conversation with your team member, concentrating solely on their developmental and growth aspirations. Within this discourse, the focal point is candidly directed toward the exploration of career advancement and personal progression, all under the aegis of the manager's guidance. This method necessitates establishing a psychologically safe workplace within the organizational context, fostering an atmosphere in which employees feel at ease openly conversing about their career objectives, even if they diverge from the manager's expectations.

A well-designed and executed career development plan with your team member can work wonders in moving an employee into a blue zone if they are playing outside of it for the majority of their work. When working with your employee, picture a road map, not just to a destination, but to a future they envision for themself. That's the essence of a career development plan.

This blueprint isn't always about climbing the corporate ladder; it's a deliberate and thoughtful strategy to cultivate the employee's skills, amplify their strengths, and navigate toward their professional aspirations. It's not etched in stone; rather, it's a dynamic guide that adapts as they learn, grow, and encounter new opportunities. By setting clear goals, seeking out experiences that stretch their abilities, and providing mentorship, you're helping them not just chart a course; you're helping them craft a narrative of their own professional evolution. A well-thought-out career development plan keeps them in the blue zone long term if they are already there, as we know that people can drift outside of their blue zone over time.

A study published in the *American Journal of Business and Management* shows that there is a high correlation between organizational environment and career development programs leading to employee job satisfaction, indicating that employees are more likely to operate in the blue zone when effective career development programs are implemented with their managers.[6]

The study concludes that "Employees start to give importance not only to financial satisfaction, but also to moral satisfaction. Given these issues, organizations that apply career management efficiently such as promotion and transfer opportunities, education and development opportunities, working conditions have become very essential for workers."[7]

Grew Fortin recommends a framework with five topic areas, which includes discussion with the employee on their development plan and aspirations on

- Your company
- Their role
- Their behavior
- Their career
- Their life

This brings about an approach of thinking holistically about their entire life rather than focusing only on work-related items.[8]

MAYBE ANOTHER ROLE

As you conduct these development and growth discussions with your employee, you may discover you're not able to offer a blue zone work environment in your team. And that is OK. People grow, and one of the natural aspects of growth may be growth in a new type of work.

Sometimes the blue zone is not in the current role but in a slightly different role within the company. A good manager and leader will recognize that and help the employee progress to that role, so they stay with the organization and continue to add value.

Lenovo, a leading PC manufacturer, does this effectively using their job rotational programs.[9] A job rotation program typically involves moving employees through different roles or departments within the company for a set period of time. This allows employees to gain a broader understanding of the organization, develop new skills, and potentially identify areas where their strengths align best.

IDENTIFYING THE RED SHIFT

Not every organization or employee is lucky to have managers who will understand and help their people grow and develop so that they work predominantly in blue zones. One of the ways in which an organization can scale their approach to identifying where these issues are is using engagement surveys and action plans.

An engagement survey can help an organization understand if, at a broad level, people at their organization are working in the blue zone or purple or red and pinpoint problems that could prevent people from being in the blue zones at a macro level.

Engagement surveys can play a valuable role in helping organizations identify when employees might not be working in their area of interest or desire. Some of the ways to do so follow.

Feedback on Tasks and Responsibilities

Engagement surveys often include questions about job satisfaction, tasks, and responsibilities. If employees consistently express dissatisfaction or lack of enthusiasm for certain tasks, it could be an indicator that they are not aligned with their interests or desired areas of work.

Interest in Future Opportunities

Surveys can inquire about employees' interest in taking on new challenges or exploring different roles. If an employee consistently shows interest in areas outside their current role, it suggests that they might be more passionate about other tasks or responsibilities.

Alignment with Goals

Engagement surveys may explore employees' alignment with the organization's mission and goals. If an employee's interests don't align with the company's objectives, it might signify a mismatch that could be addressed through a change in roles or responsibilities.

Career Development and Growth

Questions about career aspirations and growth can provide insight into whether employees see themselves growing within their current role or if they desire a shift to another area that better aligns with their ambitions.

Feedback on Team Dynamics

Surveys might include questions about team dynamics and collaboration. If an employee consistently has challenges with their team or lack of synergy, it could be related to being in a role that doesn't suit their interests.

Open-Ended Comments

Many surveys include open-ended comment sections. Employees might use these to express their preferences or suggest areas where they feel they would contribute more effectively.

Comparative Analysis

By analyzing survey results across different teams or departments, organizations can identify patterns where certain teams have higher engagement scores due to better alignment with employee interests.

Longitudinal Tracking

Over time, engagement surveys can reveal trends. If an employee's interest declines over multiple surveys, it could indicate a long-term lack of alignment.

By carefully analyzing the data collected from engagement surveys, organizations can gain insight into where employees might not be working in their desired areas of interest. This information can guide talent management strategies, including job rotations, skill development, and role changes, to create a more fulfilling work environment for employees.

For example, one such survey is Engagedly's e10, which focuses on ten key prompts that provide insight into the environment at the organization that is either helping or preventing their employees from working in the blue zone.[10] The core of the e10 survey is these ten prompts:

- I am proud of the work that I do
- I am immersed in my work
- I find the work that I do provides me with purpose and meaning
- Time flies when I'm working
- I try my hardest to perform well on my job
- I am fulfilled by the work that I do
- I am proud to work for my organization

- I am committed to doing what is required to help my organization succeed

- I would speak highly of my job and the organization to friends and colleagues

- I am willing to go above and beyond the requirements of my job to help the organization succeed

Since these surveys are done anonymously, one will not get individual-level insights, but insights at the department level or even manager level can help build an environment that allows the overall teams to move closer to a blue zone environment.

ALL HANDS

Creating a blue zone workplace, where employees excel, is a joint effort involving employees, managers, and the organization. For success, the right conditions are crucial, like supporting talent movement, regular manager check-ins that focus on both work and employee development, and a good listening tool like engagement surveys or pulse surveys to develop insights into employee aspirations, engagement, and wellness.

All three—organization, employee, and manager—play an essential role in this process. Managers need to go beyond their usual duties, conducting meaningful check-ins that cover not just tasks but also career growth and skills enhancement.

Employees, too, have a responsibility. They need to take charge of their own career progress, actively participating in skill-building and aligning personal goals with organizational aims.

Central to this is the organization, which sets the stage for growth by fostering inclusivity and providing resources. By uniting these efforts, a collaborative journey can be fostered, moving toward a blue zone workplace—a space where potential morphs into achievement and ful-fillment through combined efforts.

KEY TAKEAWAYS

- Success in talent strategy requires a deliberate effort to main-tain the blue zone where employees are engaged and fulfilled. Without intervention, entropy increases over time.

- Several factors drive people to quit, like a lack of fulfillment, a lack of growth and development, getting very little or no respect and appreciation, and a toxic workplace culture.

- The manager's role in driving a thriving, learning organizational culture involves regular check-ins, a focus on career develop-ment, job rotation for discovery and skill development, getting a pulse on employee sentiment, and driving a culture of collaboration.

9

TRANSITIONING PEOPLE OUT OF THEIR RED ZONES

There's no passion to be found in playing small—in settling
for a life that is less than the one you are capable of living.

—Nelson Mandela

I n the art world, Vincent van Gogh is revered as an icon who created masterpieces of vibrant sunflowers and starry nights. Yet, his journey to artistic greatness was not a straight one.

In his youth, van Gogh worked at the Goupil & Cie Gallery's Hague branch, meticulously packaging artworks. In 1873, he was transferred to the London branch under the direction of Charles Obach. Initially, Obach welcomed the young artist into the fold, but the welcome did not last long. Van Gogh's interactions with customers proved to be awkward, rendering him an unfit employee. He was eventually fired from his job in 1876.[1]

Van Gogh wandered for a few more years, lost without his professional connection to the art world. But by 1881, he had found his purpose in the brush. By removing van Gogh from a job he was ill-suited for, Obach had opened the door for him to put his heart and soul into his passion and improve his craft, which would transcend time and etch a place in the history books. The evocative *Starry Night* and the strokes of his self-portraits became iconic symbols of van Gogh's evolution into an artist who had found his blue zone.

Van Gogh's journey is illustrative of the path many people take. Although it can be painful in the short run to transition out of the red zones of work life, finding one's blue zones ultimately allows for the manifestation of a life and work that is fulfilling and that they excel at.

According to a research study conducted by researchers in the UK and China, there is a correlation between job stress and person–organization fit. The researchers state, "We know from prior research that [person–organization] fit bears a relation to stress. Person–environment fit theory posits that stress arises from a poor match between characteristics of the individual employee and of the job situation."[2]

There are four key components of the person–environment fit that many organizations now use to understand when a person is in a blue zone fit vs. a red zone fit for a given role: the individual's fit with the job, with the organization, within their group, and with their supervisor.

Person–Job Fit

The person–job fit focuses on the alignment of an individual's skills, abilities, and preferences with the requirements and demands of their job. When the fit is good, the individual is likely to experience lower stress and higher job satisfaction, as well as more success—better outcomes for the organization—in the role.

Person–Organization Fit

The person–organization fit considers the compatibility between an individual's values, beliefs, and work style and the values and culture of the organization. When there is a strong person–organization fit, the employee is more likely to feel a sense of belonging and satisfaction.

Person–Group Fit

Person–group fit refers to how well an individual fits within their immediate work team or group. A positive person–group fit is associated with better social integration and cooperation, reducing stress.

Person–Supervisor Fit

Person–supervisor fit focuses on the relationship between the individual and their immediate supervisor. When there is a good fit, communication and understanding are enhanced, contributing to a positive work environment.

The central idea is that when there is a poor match between the characteristics of the individual and the job or work environment, it can lead to stress and dissatisfaction. On the other hand, a good fit is associated with positive outcomes, including higher job satisfaction, better mental health, and improved performance. When there is misalignment in one or more of these dimensions and no path to getting to a good fit in these four dimensions, it is imperative that a change be made.

Ian Ziskin takes a rational view on using fit assessment to relieve someone of their role or duties, saying, "Everyone is a balance sheet, with strengths and weaknesses. When weaknesses outweigh strengths, it's time to make a change."[3]

No matter how hard it may try, a donkey cannot win the derby, and a racehorse cannot till the fields. People may want to be in a role they think they should excel in, based on their education or the title they thought the job held, only to realize that they are not quite a good fit for the role. In many cases, they may not accept or acknowledge that they were not a great fit, but their job outcomes are not what the organization wants, or the environment in which they need be in to thrive no longer exists.

In one study, "72% of American workers said they have experienced starting a new job and realizing—to their surprise or regret—that the position or company was very different from what they were led to believe."[4]

In another study, published in the *Journal of Applied Psychology*, person–organization fit perceptions were related to perceived organizational support in which supervisors are considered agents of the organization.[5] The study suggests that employees take into consideration the extent to which the organization values their effort and supports their well-being when developing a higher affinity toward increased work efforts and engagement in their role. If the role is no longer being appreciated, or their efforts are not having an impact that the organization values, then there will be a drift away from the blue zone into the red zone of work.

People change over time, and the roles they were interested in change over time, meaning it may no longer sit in their blue zone. Some people, because of their strengths and passions, may not find a blue zone in your team. In those cases, it is the role of the manager to help them transition to a different role within the organization or to work through a separation process outside the organization. It is better in some cases to transition them out of the organization and help them find their blue zone elsewhere.

MANAGERIAL MISMATCH

Sometimes misalignment comes from a manager's own actions. These are things you can control and improve in your own performance to help your team better align with their duties and the organization. In a study conducted by surveying 1,050 people who had been fired from a job, the findings were startling considering how much emphasis has been placed on employee well-being in recent times.[6]

Lack of Managerial Engagement

A staggering 75 percent of respondents disclosed that their managers had never engaged in discussions about their concerns prior to termination.[7] I was guilty of this as a young manager, when I was reticent to have hard discussions around concerns with an employee's performance. For example, if you see that the employee frequently turns in work that needs correction and changes, many inexperienced managers will endeavor to fix the errors themselves instead of using that as a coaching opportunity. Engaging with the individual, even if the manager thinks they can fix it faster instead of explaining the issue, is the right course of action.

Absence of Performance Feedback

Alarmingly, 59 percent of participants revealed that they had not received any form of performance review from their managers.[8] In the many organizations that do have a practice of performance reviews (mainly an annual one), more often than not the review process is a stressful event focused more on compliance rather than on using this as a venue for reflection on work, development, and growth for the employee.

Performance feedback is ideally more frequent and specific. Best practices, like one-on-one meetings, provide a stage to have these performance discussions. At a minimum, we recommend a quarterly check-in for employee performance and development.

Misalignment in Performance Reviews

Among those fortunate enough to have undergone a performance review, a significant 87 percent reported that there had been no indication that their employment was at risk.[9] Worse than not having a performance review is having one where the employee gets a glowing or generic review full of word salad, with no indication that their work needs improvement. This leads to an employee's perception that their performance is somewhere between perfectly acceptable and perfect. Even if there is no continuous feedback or performance check-in process, when there is one, it is incumbent upon the manager to have a candid discussion and provide feedback around the employee's performance.

Scarce Implementation of Performance Improvement Plans

A startling 90 percent of respondents disclosed that they were not placed on any type of performance improvement plan (PIP) before facing termination.[10] PIPs get a bad rap, and rightly so in many cases. Organizations and managers use PIPs as a checklist item before firing an employee. These PIPs are not really meant to drive improvement in performance but are instead a mechanism to ensure compliance with an HR process in case the organization gets sued by the employee for wrongful termination.

In an ideal world, PIPs should be completely avoidable if the manager and their direct reports have been doing frequent check-ins and performance feedback discussions. PIPs are in many ways a reflection of inconsistent or ineffective performance feedback.

In rare cases, PIPs can be an effective approach to retain and develop an otherwise good employee who may have slipped in their performance due to new skill requirements or a changing job environment. In the majority of cases, a PIP may not lead to any discernible improvement and should be used as a mechanism of last resort if there is real intent in retaining an employee and driving better outcomes.

RESOURCE MISMATCH

In today's complex organizational landscape, effective management necessitates a nuanced approach to addressing performance issues. When confronted with challenges stemming from a lack of training or resource provision, managers bear the responsibility of rectifying the situation. A well-structured development plan can be instrumental in bridging the competency gap, equipping the employee with the necessary skills and tools for success. Simultaneously, the support system must be critically examined and modified as needed to enable the employee to thrive.

Examples might include conducting individual assessments to identify the specific skills of each team member, such as programming proficiency or project management expertise. Informed by the assessment and insight into the employee's aspirations, an organization can develop training and growth programs for the team member to enhance their proficiency in the relevant area.

EMPLOYEE MISMATCH

When these factors are not at the root of the problem, it is imperative for managers to engage in candid, empathetic conversations with the employee in question. This heart-to-heart dialogue serves as a pivotal juncture to assess whether the individual is genuinely aligned with their role or if a transition to a more suitable position within the organization is warranted. Such an approach underscores the importance of both personal and organizational growth, acknowledging that a fit between employees and their roles is essential for sustained excellence and overall team success. As the business world continues to evolve, proactive, empathetic management remains the linchpin of organizational success. If there is a disconnect between what the employee thinks they are working toward and what the manager feels they should be working on, it's clear there is a mismatch of expectations. The first step for the manager is to set clear expectations.

One approach that managers and employees can take is to outline the expectations of the role and to describe what success looks like. Success needs to be something that can be validated or measured and not something that is vague in nature. Initially, the employee and the organization may be aligned, but sometimes it is clear that, as time progresses, their work may reveal that the employee is not meeting expectations. This could be for many reasons. It may be circumstantial, where the employee did not get the support and resources they needed. Or it could be because the employee did not possess the necessary skills to be successful in that role. Or it could be because the employee did not want to perform that role.

The role of the manager then becomes one of discovery with the employee to understand where the expectations and performance went off course. Understanding the reasons behind an employee's underperformance is critical. It will require a balanced and thoughtful approach from the manager. There are several strategies you can employ to uncover the root causes of an employee's underperformance to determine whether there is a problem with the skill and competence for the role or whether there is a lack of interest for the role or maybe a mismatch in alignment to the purpose and goals.

Have Open Communication

Good managers prioritize open and honest dialogue with their employees. This includes having hard conversations where you can discuss areas of improvement but also where the employee may not be suitably skilled. Engaging in regular one-on-one conversations provides a platform for employees to express their concerns, share challenges, and discuss any barriers to performance they might be facing.

Once a manager can show the employee where their performance is coming up short, they should ask questions such as, "What factors do you think might be impacting your performance, and how can I support you in overcoming any challenges you're facing?" Based on how the employee answers, the manager can delve deeper into the issues impacting their performance.

Develop Active Listening

Active listening entails not just hearing but truly comprehending what employees are saying and desiring. Sometimes what they are saying may be a good indicator of what their real desires and skills are. This involves giving full attention, asking probing questions, and seeking to understand the context and nuances of their experiences. This can provide an opportunity to really dig deep to understand where their real passion and skills lie.

An example of a probing question might be, "Are there specific tasks or projects that you find particularly challenging, and if so, what support or resources do you think would help you perform better in those areas?" The response to that question may lead to more follow-up questions to truly understand where the issues may be and if there can be a suitable approach to address them.

Track Performance Metrics

Establishing clear performance metrics and goals helps managers assess an employee's output objectively. By comparing actual results against expectations, managers can pinpoint areas that need improvement.

Unlike sales, where there are clear performance metrics, many roles in organizations may not have commonly accepted metrics. However, there are performance outcomes that can and should be tracked for each of the functions and teams. For example, for a product team, the effectiveness of the product—like customer satisfaction with the product and delivery lead time from specifications to delivery of the product—is a key metric that can be measured. For marketing, measurements on brand recall, brand affinity, and perception can be good metrics to measure the performance of that function. Metrics will vary and must be tailored to your desired outcomes; otherwise, they will drive the wrong behaviors.

Provide Feedback and Coaching

Constructive feedback and coaching are indispensable tools for manager–employee interactions. Managers should provide specific, actionable feedback that highlights strengths and identifies areas needing development.

A feedback framework such as SBI (situation, behavior, impact) can be extremely useful for providing feedback that is specific enough for an individual to take action on. An example of when to use such feedback might be when a customer expresses concern about their product not meeting their specifications. In this case, you might share this feedback with the employee: "In your recent project, I noticed that the communication with the client could have been more pro-active. To improve, consider scheduling regular check-ins to update the client on project milestones and address any concerns they may have." This directly addresses the specific problem and offers a pathway to improvement.

Do Root Cause Analysis

Experts recommend employing root cause analysis techniques, such as the Five Whys method, to delve into the underlying factors con-tributing to poor performance. This involves repeatedly asking *why* to uncover deeper layers of causation. This may help resolve whether it's a problem of training/coaching, or a deeper problem of lack of intent and passion by your employee or lack of skills and knowledge to be effective in the role.

Let's consider an example where a customer wants to cancel the order. The five whys and their answers could look like this:

Why does the customer want to cancel?
Answer: The product was defective.
Why was the product defective?
Answer: The team did deliver the product to the specifications, but the customer did not ask for that specific product.
Why did the product not have the right specifications?
Answer: The account rep did not provide the right specifications.
Why did the account rep not provide the right specifications?
Answer: The specifications were misunderstood by the account rep.

A series of such why questions may lead to an understanding of where there is a weak link in the process. In the preceding example, either the account rep was not skilled enough to fully understand and communicate the specifications or the customer miscommunicated. Doing a root cause analysis is an essential approach to understanding where the skills gaps may be.

Observation and Assessment

Managers can gain insights by observing an employee's work habits, interactions, and behaviors. This can help identify any procedural or behavioral issues that might be affecting performance.

For example, a manager may observe that an employee is frequently missing meetings or is not actively contributing to discussions in team meetings, which may signal a deeper disengagement issue.

Delve into Personal Challenges

Recognizing that external factors can impact job performance, managers should be sensitive to employees' personal challenges and offer support when needed. In some cases, the issue may be at a personal level, like someone going through a tough personal time—an illness in the family or spousal issues—that can impact their work.

Investigate Skill and Resource Gaps

Managers should assess whether an employee has the necessary skills and resources to perform their role effectively. If there are gaps, training or additional resources may be required. As in the earlier example of the customer expressing their intent to cancel an order, taking a series of whys can help one understand skill issues and address gaps in the skills with suitable training and coaching.

Ensuring Role Alignment

Ensuring that the employee's skills and strengths are aligned with their role is crucial. Misaligned roles can lead to dissatisfaction and poor performance. One effective method is doing an assessment or aspirational analysis to understand where the employee wants to grow. If there is a misalignment between the employee's self-assessment, their aspirations, and the requirements for the role, then there needs to be an honest discussion between the manager and the employee about what might have changed so that they can find an approach to better alignment.

Collaborative Problem-Solving

In some cases, involving the employee in problem-solving can yield valuable insights. Encouraging them to take an active role in finding solutions can increase engagement and ownership. In many situations, managers just tell their team members to take specific actions without involving them in the problem-solving work. Revisiting the example of the customer's intent to cancel the order, involving the team members in understanding the root cause can and should yield a better understanding of the problem and an effective solution.

Development Plans

In cases of persistent underperformance, managers might develop structured plans outlining specific actions, goals, and timelines for improvement. This establishes a clear path for the employee to regain satisfactory performance. Once the manager assesses the real issues in the underperformance, there are multiple approaches that can be taken depending on the underlying challenges or gaps in performance.

Should there be a skill or competency gap that is driving performance issues, but the employee shows the desire and aptitude to develop those skills, the manager's role then becomes to put together a development plan. The development plan helps the manager and employee to collaborate on an actionable approach for the employee to achieve their goals.

In putting forth a development goal, collaboratively set specific, measurable, achievable, relevant, and time-bound (SMART) development goals.

Ensure that these goals align with the employee's aspirations and the needs of the organization.

Clarify the roles and responsibilities of both the manager and the employee in achieving these goals. These goals should have an action plan that outlines the steps needed to achieve the agreed-upon goals. Set milestones and timelines for tracking progress. Determine how you will provide support, feedback, and coaching throughout the process.

Then, assess progress toward the development plans on a weekly basis in your one-on-one meetings.

It should be noted, however, that not all development plans work, and in that case, you may need to put the employee on a PIP or work with the employee to transition them out of the role. Remember, PIPs are a last resort action that should be avoided. They are the last action most managers take before relieving the employee of their duties. Since most PIPs result in employee termination, it may not necessarily add any real value to the process. The employee will either grow into the role or they won't. It's important to understand whether the employee is generally not a good fit because their skill, knowledge, and passion lie elsewhere.

Take a Respectful and Supportive Approach

The tone and approach you adopt are paramount. Demonstrating empathy, respect, and a genuine desire to help the employee succeed fosters trust and open communication. When you are in the process of relieving an employee of their role, realize that it is an extremely painful and personal event. Their ego is bruised, and it is imperative that the manager have a discussion with utmost care and respect. It is crucial to keep the discussion short and focused on the topic. Let the employee speak without interrupting and defending yourself. Patiently listen and offer support after the process is over. The most important thing to let them know is that this is not a reflection of them as an individual. Offer to provide a recommendation and referrals at the end of the discussion.

Help Them Move On

Transitioning an employee out of a role when they are not a good fit is a challenging but necessary aspect of being an effective manager. Research studies and best practices in this area emphasize the importance of handling such transitions with empathy, transparency, and professionalism.

The important thing is that transitioning an employee out of a role should not be a complete surprise. The amount of stress this can cause an employee can translate into depression and suicide. There is a known link between increased mortality rates and job displacement, with one research study showing double the mortality risk in a year of job loss.[11]

A good manager must take a very thoughtful and empathetic approach to an employee separation. A suggested step-by-step approach can look something like the following.

Self-Reflection and Preparation

Before the discussion, reflect on the reasons for the role transition and ensure that it is based on objective assessments and performance evaluations.

Gather relevant documentation and data that support your decision. Do not let personal bias color your judgment. Ensure that you are not using vague information and hearsay to terminate an employee. Offer concrete evidence, like that they did not consistently meet their sales targets, or that the product delivery was repeatedly delayed, or that you had several customer complaints.

Explore Alternative Roles

If there is a possible fit for the employee in another role, then it is recommended that you consider that option. There is much to be gained by the institutional knowledge this individual brings. This search for a better fit must be part of every organization's mandate. Be open to considering possible solutions, such as lateral moves or different responsibilities, if appropriate. Discuss any alternative roles within the organization that might better align with the employee's strengths and interests. Given the depth and breadth of institutional knowledge and relationships an employee has, the impact of them in a new role within the organization can be highly positive if there is proper alignment between the job responsibilities and the employee's aspirations and skills.

Choose the Right Timing

Select an appropriate time and place for the conversation, ensuring privacy and minimal disruptions. Avoid scheduling the discussion during a stressful or high-pressure period for the employee, if possible. Take the employee somewhere private, preferably at the end of the day. One of the worst feelings an employee can have happens when gathering their belongings at their desk while being watched by dozens of peering eyes. Try to do it after the day is over and most of the employees are gone, so it is less of an emotional stressor for the employee.

Be Honest and Transparent

Start the conversation by expressing your commitment to the employee's success and well-being. Clearly communicate the reasons for the role transition, focusing on specific performance or skill gaps, and back your assessment with examples and data. Be honest but compassionate in your delivery. It is imperative not to dance around the issue and to provide an honest and transparent assessment. Let the data or evidence clearly present the reasoning behind the decision.

Actively Listen and Acknowledge Feelings

Encourage the employee to share their perspective and feelings about the situation. Actively listen without interruption and acknowledge their emotions. Show empathy and understanding, but remain firm in your decision. An example would be, "I am sorry that it has gotten to this point, and I can understand how you feel."

Develop a Transition Plan

Collaborate with the employee to create a detailed transition plan that outlines the steps and timeline for the role change. Determine whether they will remain in the current role temporarily while searching for a new position or if they will be moved immediately. If possible, the organization should support a suitable transition period to minimize financial and emotional impact. Ensure that you have a thorough understanding of the activities and the impact that person has so you can have a good transition and risk-mitigation plan in place.

Before having the discussion, put together a transition plan that would look something like this:

- Activities A, B, and D will transition to Jerry, which means activities C, E, and F will transition to Ali.

- Clients X and Y will transition to Sanjay, who will need to develop a communication plan with those clients.

Offer Support and Resources

Provide resources and support to help the employee succeed in their new role or in their job search. Offer to provide a reference or assistance with networking, if they decide to explore opportunities outside the organization. As a manager or leader, you probably have contacts outside the organization to whom you can provide references. For example, you can offer to connect the employee with an external recruiter or introduce them to a peer group you are part of that may have suitable roles for them.

Maintain Confidentiality

Respect the employee's privacy and maintain confidentiality throughout the process. Ensure that discussions about the transition remain confidential unless the employee chooses to share the information. Not only are there legal issues with discussing specifics, but there may be significant impacts to organizational trust when you start talking about the specifics. When questions come up, respond to them with something like, "As you are aware, Juan is no longer with the organization, and we will not go into the details to protect the privacy and confidentiality of the individual. But if you have suggestions on how to mitigate the impact, please let me know."

Follow-Up and Check-Ins

Don't let them feel like a complete stranger, as that can have a devastating impact on their morale and self-worth. Schedule regular check-ins to monitor the employee's progress during the transition. Offer guidance, support, and feedback as needed to facilitate a smooth transition. One of the actions you can take is to call or check in with the employee during the transition—maybe meet them for a coffee or lunch—so you can understand and assist them in moving on, or offer them an ear to be supportive in their new role.

Document the Conversation

Document the discussion, including the reasons for the transition, the transition plan, and any agreed-upon actions or support measures. Share a written summary of the conversation with the employee for their reference. This ensures there is no misrepresentation of the discussion by either of you. An example of such a documentation would be something like this:

> *Sanjay, per our conversation today, your last day in your role as a design engineer will be November 21. We discussed and agreed upon a transition plan that will include you documenting all your activities and the key projects you are working on and a subsequent transition meeting with Jen to walk her through them so we can continue to support our clients effectively. Our HR team will be in touch shortly to work on the offboarding process as well as offer you support in the next phase of your career. We really appreciate everything you have contributed so far to our organization and wish you the very best. Do let me know if there is anything I can do to help.*

You can add more details if you would like, but do be sure to stay on point and not turn this documentation into a thesis.

Provide Closure

Once the transition is complete, provide closure by acknowledging the employee's contributions and expressing gratitude for their efforts. Encourage them to focus on their future growth and development.

As in the preceding example, ensure there is closure in your communication with no loose ends. There should be no ambiguity about the transition or the support the organization will offer during the transition.

Remember that handling role transitions with professionalism and empathy can help preserve the employee's dignity and maintain a positive organizational culture. It also allows the organization to better utilize its talent and resources.

In my professional experience, the decision to part ways with a job that doesn't align with one's skills, competencies, or aspirations can be a challenging and emotionally taxing experience in the short term. The uncertainty, financial impact, and emotional toll of such a transition are undeniable and real. However, it is crucial to recognize that a separation often marks the beginning of a transformative journey. In the long run, individuals who have the courage to acknowledge the alignment issues in their ill-fitting roles tend to emerge stronger and more resilient.

This adversity can often serve as a catalyst for personal growth, pushing individuals to reevaluate their career paths, rediscover their true strengths, and seek opportunities that resonate with their passions and ambitions. It is within these better-fitting roles that individuals not only find professional fulfillment but also unlock their full potential. In environments where their skills and values align with the demands of the job, they are more likely to thrive, excel, and ultimately become the best versions of themselves.

So, while the decision to leave from a misaligned job may feel like a leap into the unknown, it often paves the way for a brighter and more fulfilling future where one can flourish and make a lasting impact.

KEY TAKEAWAYS

- Relieving an employee from an organization is a very stressful event for the employee but also for the manager. Before making this decision, a thorough review and action steps must be taken, such as an assessment of what's driving the lack of performance, delving into personal challenges, and making accommodations, if possible.

- Once a decision is made to relieve an employee, do so with utmost compassion for the individual. Offer support, such as exploring different roles within the organization where the employee may thrive, or provide recommendations for roles outside the organization.

- Sometimes leaving the organization opens up new opportunities for the individual, where they discover their true calling for the work that they enjoy and are skilled at, finding a career that offers an ikigai workplace.

ACKNOWLEDGMENTS

Writing a book is a labor of love, a journey that often stretches beyond the bounds of a single author's efforts. It is with deep gratitude and a sense of profound appreciation that I acknowledge the individuals and their experiences and inspirations that have contributed to the creation of this work.

First and foremost, I extend my heartfelt gratitude to the Okinawan people, whose concept of ikigai provided the foundational philosophy for this book. Their wisdom and approach to life, work, and relationships have illuminated the path to purpose and fulfillment for countless individuals, including myself. It is a privilege to share their insights with a wider audience.

Viktor Frankl's seminal work on the pursuit of meaning in life and work has been a guiding light throughout my philosophy, reflected in my work. His words continue to resonate deeply within me, reminding us all of the innate human desire for purpose and personal growth.

Master Chef Jiro's inspiring journey, dedicated to making the best sushi, is a great analogy on how we should think about work.

I wouldn't be the human I am without the sacrifice and guidance my parents gave me, while expecting so little in return. So thank you, Appa and Amma, for raising me and guiding my values in life.

To the many leaders, mentors, colleagues, and employees I have had the privilege of working with over the years, I extend my sincerest gratitude. Your experiences, guidance, and shared insights have enriched my understanding of ikigai in the context of the workplace. It is through our collaborations and interactions that I have been able to put those practices to work in my life as CEO and founder of my small start-up, Engagedly, over the years.

I want to express my profound appreciation for the Engagedly team and our customers. Our team's insatiable appetite for learning, passion for work, and teamwork have led to creating a positive workplace culture and fostering individual growth, which has inspired me greatly. I have been fortunate to lead a team that would be the envy of many organizations worldwide. Some of the key people are my partners at Engagedly, who have inspired and contributed to my personal growth and my practice of ikigai at work—namely, Jay Shankar, Aaron Adams, Pankaj Singh, and many more whom I cannot possibly name here who have played their part.

Engagedly has been a remarkable platform for translating the principles of ikigai into real-world practice with our customers, and I am grateful for the opportunity to learn from this exceptional community.

I want to express deep gratitude to my mentor Gordon Rapkin, who recently retired as CEO of a technology company, for bestowing upon me his wisdom in running and growing five different organizations over his long, illustrious career.

I am very appreciative of many of the leaders and CEOs who contributed to this book—namely, Melissa Widner, CEO of Lighter Capital; Wendy Hamilton, CEO of Techsmith; Ian Ziskin, former CHRO of Northrup Grumman; Edie Goldberg, PhD, future-of-work thought leader; Matt Poepsel, PhD, godfather of performance optimization; and Drew Fortin, CEO of Lever Talent.

Finally, to Nathan True, my manuscript development editor with Greenleaf Books, without whom this book would not have been possible. Without his continuous review, encouragement, and prodding, I probably would have abandoned this project several times.

My family, friends, and loved ones have been unwavering sources of support, encouragement, and understanding throughout this journey. Your belief in the importance of purpose and your continuous encouragement have been my driving force. I am deeply grateful for your presence in my life, especially my daughter, Saachi, who kept prodding me with statements like "Shouldn't you be working on your book instead of watching Netflix?," reminding me to invest those late evenings and early mornings to finish my book.

To the readers of this book, I extend my warmest appreciation. It is your curiosity, open-mindedness, and willingness to explore the concept of ikigai that bring this work to life. I hope these pages provide you with valuable insights and practical guidance for finding purpose and fulfillment in your own careers and lives.

Finally, I want to acknowledge the countless authors, researchers, and thought leaders who have contributed to the field of personal and organizational development. Your work has laid the foundation for the ideas and principles presented in this book. I stand on the shoulders of giants, and I am grateful for the wisdom you have shared with the world.

In closing, I recognize that the pursuit of ikigai is a journey that continues for all of us. May we all find the courage to seek our purpose, the perseverance to align our passions and skills, and the commitment to contribute to meaningful missions in the world. Together, we can create workplaces and lives filled with purpose, joy, and fulfillment.

With gratitude,
Sri Chellappa

WORKBOOK

This is a short workbook to assess the ikigai zone of your team member. There is nothing scientific about this, so you may wish to edit this approach to suit your culture and team dynamics.

Assessing the ikigai zone is a two-step process: The first step is getting input from the employee about their own perception and views of their work. The second step is getting that validated and mapped to the manager's perception of the employee's work. The suggested rating method that follows can then tell you which zone the employee is in. The one very important aspect of this exercise is that there must be trust between these two people. Without it, you may not get honest responses from the employee, and that faulty data would invalidate this exercise.

To complete this workbook, run a survey with the following outline:

- Ask the employee for the top ten work activities they perform in their current role.

- Ask them to rank these ten work activities by time spent in an average week or month on these activities.

- Ask them to rate on a scale of 1–4 their perception of their skill level in these activities.

- Ask them to rate on a scale of 1–4 their desire or how much they enjoy doing these activities.

Once the manager gets this table, it will be their turn to rate:

- Each activity on your assessment of their skill level on a scale of 1–4.

- Each activity on your assessment of the value it adds to the company on a scale of 1–4.

FINAL CALCULATION

The first step is normalizing the skill score between the employee score and the manager score. I recommend you average the two scores, so there is less bias toward either the manager or the employee in the final skill score.

The second step is calculating the final composite score using a weighted scoring method, which involves several steps. First, calculate the nominal score for each activity by adding the three areas: score on desire, average skill score, and value to the organization. The maximum score for each activity is 12. Then multiply each activity score by the activity weight. The first activity listed has the highest weight of 10, the second activity has the weight of 9, and so on until the last activity, which has a weight of 1. Finally, sum all the weighted scores. The maximum score on the activity score for the first activity is 120 (10 × 12), for the second activity it is 108 (9 × 12), and so on until the last activity, which has a maximum score of 12. The total maximum score possible is 660.

Assessing the Ikigai Zone

There are many ways to assess the ikigai zone score, but a simple approach I suggest is a total score higher than 528 (80 percent of 660) for an employee to be working in the blue zone. The higher, the better, obviously. Scores below 400 should be cause for alarm, because there is a strong probability that the individual is in the red zone, and you should take a corrective approach as laid out in this book.

Here is an example of ikigai zone scoring for an individual in the marketing analyst role, which provides an illustration of how to calculate the scores.

Weight	Activity	Employee's Desire	Employee's Self Skill Assessment	Manager's Skill Assessment	Skill Average	Value to the Org	Total Nominal Score	Weighted Score
10	Writing blogs	3	3	2	2.5	2	7.5	75
9	Optimizing SEO on page	2	2	2	2	3	7	63
8	Social media management	2	3	2	2.5	2	6.5	52
7	Working on animations	4	4	2	3	2	9	63
6	Research competitors	3	3	2	2.5	1	6.5	39
5	Fix old blogs	1	4	4	4	2	7	35
4	Respond to comments online	1	4	4	4	2	7	28
3	Video production and editing	4	4	2	3	3	10	30
2	Email marketing	4	4	2	3	4	11	22
1	Producing webinars	4	4	2	3	4	11	11
							Total Score	418

In this example, the person is clearly spending a lot of time in activities that they don't enjoy and are not very skilled at. Additionally, the value to the organization is not the highest in those activities. This leads to an overall suboptimal score of 418 out of maximum 660. Clearly, this person is not working in an ikigai blue zone. Upon further review, it is evident that there are quite a few activities that are in the blue zone, where the desire, skill, and value to the organization are high but the amount of time spent in this zone is not. The manager and employee can work together to adjust their work by either removing some of the other activities that are less valuable to the organization or shifting those activities to other team members who may be more skilled at them. The approach taken by the team will vary based on the scores of other individuals and the overall goals of the team and the organization.

This is an example of how to assess the ikigai zone, but realize that this is just a high-level approach to fostering a conversation. One simple way to implement this workbook is to use a survey tool or Google Forms combined with Google Sheets or Excel to calculate the score.

I have included a blank assessment sheet for your convenience.

Weight	Activity	Employee's Desire	Employee's Self Skill Assessment	Manager's Skill Assessment	Skill Average	Value to the Org	Total Nominal Score	Weighted Score
							Total Score	

NOTES

1. THE IKAGI BLUE ZONE AND WORKPLACE

1. Wendy Hamilton, email response to author interview questionnaire, June 26, 2023.
2. "The Most and Least Meaningful Jobs." Payscale, https://www.payscale.com/data-packages/most-and-least-meaningful-jobs/full-list.
3. "Employee Engagement." Gallup, https://www.gallup.com/394373/indicator-employee-engagement.aspx.

2. WHAT THE PERSON IS GOOD AT

1. Benjamin Bloom, *Developing Talent in Young People* (New York: Random House, 1985).
2. K. Anders Ericsson, Ralf Th. Krampe, and Clemens Tesch-Romer, "The Role of Deliberate Practice in the Acquisition of Expert Performance," *Psychological Review* 100, no. 3 (1993): 363–406, https://doi.org/10.1037/0033-295X.100.3.363.
3. Malcolm Gladwell, *Outliers* (Boston: Little, Brown and Company, 2008).
4. Ola Svenson, "Are We All Less Risky and More Skillful Than Our Fellow Drivers?" *Acta Psychologica* 47 (1981): 143–148, https://gwern.net/doc/psychology/1981-svenson.pdf.
5. Justin Kruger and David Dunning, "Unskilled and Unaware of It: How Difficulties in Recognizing One's Own Incompetence Lead to Inflated Self-Assessments," *Journal of Personality and Social Psychology* 77, no. 6 (1999): 1121–1134, https://doi.org/10.1037/0022-3514.77.6.1121.

6. Gordon Rapkin, email response to author interview questionnaire, June 22, 2023.

7. *This Is It*, directed by Kenny Ortega (Sony Pictures, 2009).

8. Matt Poepsel, email response to author interview questionnaire, July 8, 2023.

9. Naomi Osaka, press conference at the 2021 French Open, June 2021.

10. Kim Parker and Juliana Menasce Horowitz, "Majority of Workers Who Quit a Job in 2021 Cite Low Pay, No Opportunities for Advancement, Feeling Disrespected," Pew Research, March 9, 2022, https://www.pewresearch.org/short-reads/2022/03/09/majority-of-workers-who-quit-a-job-in-2021-cite-low-pay-no-opportunities-for-advancement-feeling-disrespected/.

11. Drew Fortin, email response to author interview questionnaire, July 10, 2023.

3. WHAT THE PERSON IS PASSIONATE ABOUT

1. Jeremy Bauer-Wolf, "Don't Find Your Passion—Cultivate It, Psychologists Say," Inside Higher Ed, July 23, 2018, https://www.insidehighered.com/news/2018/07/24/study-creating-your-passions-more-effective-finding-them.

2. Paul O'Keefe, Carol Dweck, and Gregory Walton, "Implicit Theories of Interest: Finding Your Passion or Developing It?" *Psychological Science* 29, no. 10 (October 2018), https://www.ncbi.nlm.nih.gov/pmc/articles/PMC6180666/.

3. Wendy Hamilton, email response to author interview questionnaire, June 26, 2023.

4. Michelle French-Holloway, *A New Meaning-Mission Fit* (New York: Spring, 2020).

5. "Fauja Singh," Wikipedia, January 20, 2024, https://en.wikipedia.org/wiki/Fauja_Singh.

6. Drew Fortin, email response to author interview questionnaire, July 10, 2023.

7. Cecilie Schou Andreassen, Holger Ursin, and Hege R. Eriksen, "The Relationship between Strong Motivation to Work, 'Workaholism,' and Health," *Psychology & Health* 22, no. 5 (2007), 615–629.

8. Michael Kardas and Ed O'Brien, "Easier Said Than Done: Merely Watching Others Perform Can Foster an Illusion of Skill Acquisition," *Psychological Science* 29, no. 4 (February 2018), https://doi.org/10.1177/0956797617740646.

9. Edie Goldberg, email response to author interview questionnaire, July 5, 2023.

4. WHAT THE ORGANIZATION VALUES AND NEEDS

1. "Purpose," Walmart, accessed March 1, 2024, https://corporate.walmart.com/purpose.

2. "Our Mission," United Way, accessed March 1, 2024, https://www.unitedway.org/our-impact/mission#.

3. "Public Service Commission of Canada," Government of Canada, accessed March 1, 2024, https://www.canada.ca/en/public-service-commission.html.

4. Ian Ziskin, email response to author interview questionnaire, June 28, 2023.

5. Edie Goldberg, email response to author interview questionnaire, July 5, 2023.

6. Sue Cantrell, Robin Jones, Michael Griffiths, and Julie Hiipakka, "The Skills-Based Organization: A New Operating Model for Work and the Workforce," *Deloitte Insights*, Issue 31, September 8, 2022, https://www2.deloitte.com/us/en/insights/topics/talent/organizational-skill-based-hiring.html.

7. Cantrell et al., "The Skills-Based Organization."

8. "Managing in a VUCA World," MindTools, https://www.mindtools.com/asnydwg/managing-in-a-vuca-world.

9. Ravin Jesuthasan and John Boudreau, *Work without Jobs* (Cambridge, MA: The MIT Press, 2022).

5. YOUR CULTURE CIRCLE

1. "Understanding and Developing Organizational Culture," Society for Human Resource Management (SHRM), https://www.shrm.org/resourcesandtools/tools-and-samples/toolkits/pages/understandinganddevelopingorganizationalculture.aspx

2. Wendy Hamilton, email response to author interview questionnaire, June 26, 2023.

3. Ian Ziskin, email response to author interview questionnaire, June 28, 2023.

4. Melissa Widner, email response to author interview questionnaire, June 22, 2023.

5. Davan Maharaj, "Sunbeam Gives the Ax to CEO 'Chainsaw Al,'" *LA Times*, June 16, 1998, https://www.latimes.com/archives/la-xpm-1998-jun-16-mn-60340-story.html.

6. "Our People and Culture," FedEx, https://www.fedex.com/en-us/about/who-we-are.html.

7. Brie Weiler Reynolds, "FlexJobs, Mental Health America Survey: Mental Health in the Workplace," Flexjobs, https://www.flexjobs.com/blog/post/flexjobs-mha-mental-health-workplace-pandemic/.

8. Eric Garton, "Employee Burnout Is a Problem with the Company, Not the Person," *Harvard Business Review*, April 6, 2017, https://hbr.org/2017/04/employee-burnout-is-a-problem-with-the-company-not-the-person.

9. Michael Mankins and Eric Garton, *Time, Talent, Energy* (Brighton, MA: Harvard Business Review Press, 2017).

10. Alexa Mikhail, "Spotify Gives Workers a Paid Week off to Recharge," *Fortune*, November 1, 2022, https://fortune.com/well/2022/11/01/spotify-gives-workers-a-paid-wellness-week/.

6. FINDING THE BLUE ZONE

1. Victor Frankl, *Man's Search for Meaning* (London: Rider, 2011).

2. Frankl, *Man's Search*.

3. Frankl, Man's Search.

4. Frankl, Man's Search.

5. Frankl, Man's *Search*, 166.

6. Nina McQueen, "Workplace Culture Trends: The Key to Hiring (and Keeping) Top Talent in 2018," *LinkedIn* (blog), LinkedIn, June 26, 2018, https://www.linkedin.com/blog/member/career/workplace-culture-trends-the-key-to-hiring-and-keeping-top-talent.

7. Frank Martela and Anne B. Pessi, "Significant Work Is about Self-Realization and Broader Purpose: Defining the Key Dimensions of Meaningful Work," *Frontiers in Psychology* 9 (March 2018).

8. Simon Sinek, *Start with the Why* (New York: Portfolio, 2009), 94.

9. Erik Berggren and Rob Bernshteyn, "Organizational Transparency Drives Company Performance," *Journal of Management Development* 26, no. 5 (May 2007).

7. HIRING FOR THE BLUE ZONE

1. Lisa Frye, "The Cost of a Bad Hire Can be Astronomical," SHRM, May 9, 2017, https://www.shrm.org/topics-tools/news/employee-relations/cost-bad-hire-can-astronomical.

2. Falon Fatemi, "The True Cost of a Bad Hire—It's More Than You Think," *Forbes*, September 28, 2016, https://www.forbes.com/sites/falonfatemi/2016/09/28/the-true-cost-of-a-bad-hire-its-more-than-you-think/?sh=26475faf4aa4.

3. Ben Goldberg, "75% of Employers Have Hired the Wrong Person, Here's How to Prevent That," CareerBuilder, https://resources.careerbuilder.com/news-research/prevent-hiring-the-wrong-person.

4. Matt Poepsel, email response to author interview questionnaire, July 8, 2023.

5. Lou Adler, *Hire with Your Head* (Hoboken, NJ: Wiley, 2021).

6. Adler, *Hire with Your Head.*

7. Adler, Hire with Your Head.

8. Adler, Hire with Your Head.

9. Adler, Hire with Your Head.

10. Adler, Hire with Your Head.

11. Adler, Hire with Your Head.

12. Gordon Rapkin, email response to author interview questionnaire, June 22, 2023.

8. DEVELOPING PEOPLE FOR THE BLUE ZONE

1. Matt Poepsel, email response to author interview questionnaire, July 8, 2023.

2. Timothy Judge and John Kammeyer-Mueller, "Job Attitudes," *Annual Review of Psychology* 63 (January 2012): 341–367.

3. Russell Cropanzano and Marie Mitchell, "Social Exchange Theory: An Interdisciplinary Review," *Journal of Management* 31, no. 6 (December 2005): 874–900.

4. Edward Deci and Richard Ryan, "The 'What' and 'Why' of Goal Pursuits: Human Needs and the Self-Determination of Behavior," *Psychological Inquiry* 11, no. 4 (2000): 227–268.

5. Jari Hakanen, Riku Perhoniemi, and Salla Toppinen-Tanner, "Positive Gain Spirals at Work: From Job Resources to Work Engagement, Personal Initiative and Work-Unit Innovativeness," *Journal of Vocational Behavior* 73, no. 1 (August 2008): 78–91.

6. Çiğdem Kaya and Belgin Ceylan, "An Empirical Study on the Role of Career Development Programs in Organizations and Organizational Commitment on Job Satisfaction of Employees," *American Journal of Business and Management* 3, no. 3 (2014): 178–191, http://worldscholars.org/index.php/ajbm/article/view/551/pdf.

7. Kaya and Ceylan, "An Empirical Study."

8. Drew Fortin, email response to author interview questionnaire, July 10, 2023.

9. Danielle Murdaugh, "Case Study: How Lenovo Uses a Job Rotational Program to Train and Retain Top Young Talent," *Workforce Development*, Training Industry, August 18, 2022, https://trainingindustry.com/articles/workforce-development/case-study-how-lenovo-uses-a-job-rotational-program-to-train-and-retain-top-young-talent.

10. "What is Engagedly's e10 Survey and Its Uses?" Engagedly, https://engagedly.com/product/e10-engagement-survey/.

9. TRANSITIONING PEOPLE OUT OF THEIR RED ZONES

1. Meilan Solly, "Employer Who Pushed van Gogh to New Career Path Revealed in Studio Photo," *Smithsonian Magazine*, October 23, 2018, https://www.smithsonianmag.com/smart-news/man-who-fired-vincent-van-gogh-his-only-steady-art-world-job-180970604/.

2. Pei Chen, Paul Sparrow, and Cary Cooper, "The Relationship between Person-Organization Fit and Job Satisfaction," *Journal of Managerial Psychology* 31, no. 5 (2016): 946–959, https://www.emerald.com/insight/content/doi/10.1108/JMP-08-2014-0236/full/html.

3. Ian Ziskin, email response to author interview questionnaire, June 28, 2023.

4. Devin Tomb, "72% of Muse Survey Respondents Say They've Experienced 'Shift Shock,'" *The Muse*, August 30, 2022, https://www.themuse.com/advice/shift-shock-muse-survey-2022.

5. Robert Eisenberger, Robin Huntington, Steven Hutchison, and Debora Sowa, "Perceived organizational support," *Journal of Applied Psychology* 71, no.3 (1986): 500–507, https:// https://doi.org/10.1037/0021-9010.71.3.500.

6. Jen Fisher and Paul Silverglate, "The C-Suite's Role in Well-Being," Deloitte Insights, June 22, 2022, https://www2.deloitte.com/xe/en/insights/topics/leadership/employee-wellness-in-the-corporate-workplace.html.

7. Fisher and Silverglate, "The C-Suite."

8. Fisher and Silverglate, "The C-Suite."

9. Fisher and Silverglate, "The C-Suite."

10. Fisher and Silverglate, "The C-Suite."

11. Timothy Classen and Richard Dunn, "The Effect of Job Loss and Unemployment Duration on Suicide Risk in the United States: A New Look Using Mass-Layoffs and Unemployment Duration," *Health Economics* 21, no. 3 (Mar 2012): 338–350, https://www.ncbi.nlm.nih.gov/pmc/articles/PMC3423193.

ABOUT THE AUTHOR

SRI CHELLAPPA, cofounder and CEO of Engagedly, is a passionate entrepreneur, filmmaker, musician, and people leader. He has spent almost thirty years leading technology teams, as well as teams in music and film. He has a unique background in software, people management, health care, film writing, directing, and producing, and running a recording studio. Sri brings diverse experiences across industries and specialties to build high-performing, highly engaged organizations.

Sri is also an author, producer, and director of six feature films; producer of two music EPs with his prog rock band Manchester Underground; and manager of a recording studio in St. Louis. Additionally, he is the host of *The People Strategy Leaders* podcast, which focuses on interviewing people leaders and their practices in the future of work.

His writings and his thoughts on leading people to achieve great things can be accessed on LinkedIn at https://www.linkedin.com/in/srikantchellappa.